2-6-75

THE PSALMS FOR WORSHIP TODAY

Dwight W. Vogel

Publishing House
St. Louis   London

ACKNOWLEDGEMENTS

This work is partly due to my father's contagious love of the psalms. That love was strengthened by the teaching of John Scammon during my seminary days at Andover-Newton. The preparation of weekly services for the Vespers community at Westmar intensified my sense of need for using psalms meaningfully in worship.

Daily prayers with the monks at St. John's and the nuns of St. Benedict's Convent, St. Joseph, Minn., reminded me of how rich a heritage Protestants were using so inadequately. The encouragement of the American Bible Society was an additional incentive to continue and complete the work.

To all of the above, and especially to my colleagues at the Institute, go my sincere thanks. For my wife Linda, whose interest, advice, and continual help are evident on every page of this work, there can be no adequate expression of appreciation. Her love, her scholarly insights, her willingness to assist with even the most tedious chores connected with this project have been channels of God's grace.

Westmar College, Lent 1974

The Bible text in this publication is from *The Psalms for Modern Man* in Today's English Version. Copyright © American Bible Society, 1970. Used by permission.

Concordia Publishing House, St. Louis, Missouri
Concordia Publishing House Ltd., London, E. C. 1
Copyright © 1974 Concordia Publishing House

MANUFACTURED IN THE UNITED STATES OF AMERICA

Library of Congress Cataloging in Publication Data

Bible. O. T. Psalms. English. Today's English.
    Selections. 1974.
    The psalms for worship today.

    I. Vogel, Dwight W., comp. II. Title.
BS1436.V6   223'.2'052   74-13761
ISBN 0-570-03239-3

CONTENTS

THE PSALMS FOR WORSHIP TODAY

The psalms have been used in worship for well over 2,000 years. Related closely to the worship of the Jerusalem temple, they were an essential part of synagog life. Later they provided the early church with its basic hymnbook.

Through the ages the psalms have remained a constant treasury of sources for use in worship. Every liturgical revival and every period of church renewal has rediscovered the psalms as important to the life of the worshiping community. They have been the predominant source for community prayer by religious orders, and their imagery has colored hymnody.

Yet in our day much of the vitality of the psalms goes unappropriated. In many experimental services they go unused, to the poverty of the participants. In many services where they are used, they seem to lack power and significance. As one involved in preparing weekly liturgies, I have had to ask "Why?"

3

One answer is found in a language which does not speak as the participants speak. The wording of the King James Version, while beautiful in its own right, is far removed from our way of expressing ourselves even when at our literary best. Subsequent versions have corrected the most obvious misunderstandings, but have left the basic style in Tudor English.

A second answer is that in a day when allegory has limited use, some passages do not express and form the convictions of the Christian community at all. When in a psalm of praise we read, "You have condemned the heathen and destroyed the wicked, and they will be remembered no more" (Ps. 9:5), our voices catch. On the face of it, such a statement is inconsistent with our view of God. On further examination and study the passage gains meaning since the wicked "digs a deep hole in the ground, then falls into his own pit!" (Ps. 7:15)

But psalms used in worship are not the occasion for study and historical interpretation. Rather they spring from the depth of the whole person and gain power and usefulness for worship through immediate understanding. They function as forms for the communal expression of these convictions. Implications must be explicit, with a minimum of rational interpretation required. This does not mean that the mind cannot be at work in worship, but rather that community expressions rely on first impressions. The service moves on, and it moves on without us if we are forced to stop and figure out the meaning of what we are saying. There are appropriate places in worship for this kind of thinking to take place (e. g., the contemporary word or sermon). While we need not understand the full depth of what we say as a community (after 19 centuries we are still discovering the richness of the Lord's Prayer), the immediate connotation of what we are saying together should be clear and honest.

A third problem confronted in the contemporary use of the psalms in worship is the sudden change of mood in many psalms. A plea for help may suddenly shift to an affirmation of praise (e. g., Ps. 28). Scholars help us understand that between the two sections a priest may have given "words of assurance." We do not have his lines but only the response to them. It may, thus, recapture the original use of the psalms to separate parts of one psalm in a contemporary worship service.

A fourth problem is the somewhat rigid way in which psalms have been pushed into exactly the same position in every worship service no matter what the psalm being used was saying. Many have shared the experience of reading a cry for help or a confession of sin in the position of an act of praise. Sometimes our participation in the service never quite recovers!

Finally, psalms are usually read antiphonally either between liturgists and congregation or with one part of the community responding to another. That is the way psalms should be used in worship. Unfortunately, in the transmission and translation of the text as we have it, this is sometimes cumbersome and breaks the natural meaning.

Here these problems have been taken into account. Our aim has been to provide a contemporary psalter which can express the deepest needs, the highest hopes, and the most significant commitments of the worshiping community.

To counteract the problem of archaic language, we have used Today's English Version, which makes use of contemporary language while maintaining a reverence for the text.

We have tried to provide a resource which will speak to and from the Christian community today. Thus we have omitted passages which are particularly difficult to understand, which seem sub-Christian, or which are cumbersome for liturgical use. This work should not, therefore, be used as the basis for a study of the psalms in their historical and Biblical context. This is a book of resources for worship, not an edition of the Book of Psalms.

It is our hope that the Holy Spirit will be able to use this work to enable the psalms once again to speak to and for us in our worship.

SUGGESTIONS FOR USE

These psalms are arranged according to the place they might fill in contemporary worship. A psalm has been separated when there is a dominant change of mood. Some psalms are used both in their complete form and with specific excerpts (e. g., Ps. 77 appears as a psalm of supplication, while verses 1-2, 11-12 appear separately as a call to prayer and celebration). If all or almost all of the psalm is used, the heading gives the chapter only (e. g., "19"). If the reading is composed of excerpts from a psalm, the opening verse is indicated (e. g., "11:1" or "19:7").

These psalms may be read in various ways. In some communities of worship a liturgist will read those lines in regular print while the community will respond with those in italic type. Or, one group of the congregation may read one part while the rest of the community responds with the other. (Possible divisions include choir and congregation, community left and right of the center aisle, men and women, young people and adults.) There has been no attempt to be consistent in this arrangement by always having parallel lines answer each other or by letting the arbitrary verse division dictate the changing voice. We have sought rather to let the text speak in the most natural and meaningful way.

A third possibility designates lines for the liturgist or leader (L), two groups which may be divided in any one of the above ways (designated 1 and 2), and unison sections (designated by U).

All uses of each psalm may be found in the index. If you wish to use the entire psalm, select the one with a chapter designation only.

A lectionary for daily prayer enabling the user to read through most of the psalms in 8 weeks, is available from the publisher of this book on request.

The church year lectionary has references related to the recent 3-year cycle being used by an increasing number of denominations. Readings for a Season of God the Father (celebrated during the 8 weeks prior to Advent) are included for those of us who have found this variation on the traditional church year meaningful.

INDEX

CALLS TO
PRAYER AND CELEBRATION

18:1

L: How I love you, Lord!

1: *You are my defender.*
The Lord is my Savior;
he is my strong fortress.
My God is my protection,
and I am safe with him.
He protects me like a shield;
he defends me and keeps me safe.

2: Death pulled its ropes tight around me;
the waves of destruction rolled over me.
Death pulled its ropes tight around me,
and the grave set its trap for me.
In my trouble I called to the Lord;
I called to my God for help.
In his temple he heard my voice;
my cry for help reached his ears.

U: *Praise the Lord!*

18:31

L: The Lord alone is God;

U: *God alone is our defense.*

1: He is the God who makes me strong,
who makes my pathway safe.
He makes me surefooted as a deer;
he keeps me safe on the mountains.
He trains me for battle,
so that I can use the strongest bow.

8

2: You, Lord, protect me and save me;
your care has made me great,
and your power has kept me safe.

18:46

L: The Lord lives! Praise my defender!

1: *God is my Savior! Proclaim his greatness!*
He gives me victory over my enemies;
he saves me from my foes.

2: You, Lord, give me victory over my enemies
and protect me from violent men.
So I will praise you among the nations;
I will sing praise to you.

U: He shows constant love to the one he has chosen,
to David and his descendants forever.

21:13

L: Come, Lord, with your strength!

U: *We will sing and praise your power.*

34:1

L: I will always thank the Lord;

U: *I will never stop praising him.*

L: I will praise him for what he has done;

U: *may all who are oppressed listen and be glad!*

L: Proclaim with me the Lord's greatness;

U: *let us praise his name together!*

35:9

L: I will be glad because of the Lord;

U: *I will be happy because he saved me.*

L: With all my heart I will say to the Lord,
"There is no one like you!"

U: *"You protect the weak from the strong,*
the poor and needy from the oppressor!"

1: I will thank you in the large assembly,
I will praise you before a great crowd.

2: May those who are glad that I am acquitted
shout with joy and say again and again,
"Great is the Lord;
he is happy with the success of his servant!"

U: Then I will proclaim your righteousness,
and I will praise you all day long.

40:13

L: Save me, Lord! Help me now!

U: *May all who come to you be glad and joyful!*
L: May all who love your salvation always say,

U: *"How great the Lord is!"*

41:10

L: Be merciful to me, Lord,

U: *and restore my health;*

1: You will help me;

2: *you will keep me in your presence forever.*

L: Let us praise the Lord, the God of Israel;

U: *praise him now and forever! Amen! Amen!*

47:5

L: God goes up to his throne!

U: *There are shouts of joy and the blast of trumpets*
as the Lord goes up!

L: Sing praise to God;

U: *sing praise to our king!*

L: God is king over all the world;

U: *praise him with songs!*

51:10

L: Create a pure heart in me, God,
and put a new and loyal spirit in me.

1: Do not banish me from your presence;
   do not take your Holy Spirit away from me.
   Give me again the joy that comes from your salvation,
   and make my spirit obedient.

2: *Help me to speak, Lord, and I will praise you.*
   You do not want sacrifices, or I would offer them;
   You are not pleased with burnt offerings.

U: *My sacrifice is a submissive spirit, God;*
   a submissive and obedient heart you will not reject.

62:5

L: I depend on God alone;
   I put my hope in him.

1: He alone is my protector and Savior;
   he is my defender, and I shall never be defeated.

2: My salvation and honor depend on God;
   he is my strong protector; he is my shelter.

L: My people, trust in God at all times!

U: *Tell him all your troubles, because he is our refuge.*

66:1

L: Praise God with shouts of joy, all people!

U: *Sing to the glory of his name;*
   offer him glorious praise!

L: Come and see what God has done,
   his wonderful acts among men.

U: *Sing to the glory of his name;*
   offer him glorious praise!
   Say to God, "How wonderful are the things you do!"

67

L: God, be merciful to us and bless us;

U: *look on us with kindness,*
   that the whole world may know your will;
   that all nations may know your salvation.

1: May the peoples praise you, God;

2:   *may all peoples praise you!*

1: May the nations be glad and sing for joy,
   because you judge the peoples with justice
   and guide all the nations.

2:   *May the peoples praise you, God;*

1:   *may all peoples praise you!*

2: God, our God, has blessed us.

U: *God has blessed us;*
     may all people everywhere honor him.

68:3

L: The righteous will be glad
   and rejoice in God's presence;

U: *they will be exceedingly happy.*

1: Sing to God, sing praise to his name;
     prepare a way for him who rides on the clouds.

2: His name is the Lord—
     be glad in his presence!

68:19

L: Praise the Lord, who carries our burdens day after day;

U: *he is the God who saves us.*

1: Our God is a God who saves;

2:   *he is the Lord, our Lord, who rescues us from death.*

68:32

L: Sing to God, kingdoms of the world,

1: sing praise to the Lord,
   to him who rides in the sky, the ancient sky!
     Listen to him shout with a mighty roar!

2: Proclaim God's power;
     his majesty is over Israel,
     his might is in the skies.

1: How wonderful is God in his sanctuary,
   the God of Israel!

2:   *He gives strength and power to his people.*

U: *Praise God!*

70:1

L: Save me, God!
   Lord, help me now!

1: May all who come to you be glad and joyful!

2:   *May all who love your salvation always say,*
     "How great God is!"

71:22

L: I will indeed praise you;

1:   *I will praise your faithfulness, my God.*
     I will play hymns to you, the Holy One of Israel.

2: I will shout for joy as I play for you;
   with my whole being I will sing,
   because you have saved me.

72:18

L: Praise the Lord, the God of Israel,
   who alone does these wonderful things!

U: *Praise his glorious name forever,*
     and may his glory fill the whole earth!

1: Amen!

2:   *Amen!*

77:1

L: I cry aloud to God;
   I cry aloud, and he hears me.

1: In time of trouble I pray to the Lord;
   all night long I lift my hands in prayer.

2: I will remember your great acts, Lord;
   I will recall the wonders you did in the past.
   I will think about all that you have done;
   I will meditate on all your deeds.

81:1

L: Shout with joy to God our defender;
  sing praises to the God of Jacob!

1: Start the music and play the tambourines;
  Play pleasant music on the harps and the lyres.
  Blow the horn for the festival;
  when the moon is new, and when the moon is full,
  shout with joy.

2: Listen, my people, to my warning;
  Israel, how I wish you would listen to me!
  You must never serve or worship anyone else but me.

U: I am the Lord, your God,
  who brought you out of the land of Egypt.
  Open your mouth, and I will feed you.

84:1

L: How I love your temple, Almighty God!
  How I want to be there!

2: I long for the courts of the Lord's temple.
  With my whole being I sing with joy to the living God.

1: Even the sparrows have built a nest,
  and the swallows have their own home;

  they keep their young near your altars,
  Lord Almighty, my king and my God.

U: *How happy are those who live in your temple,*
  always singing praise to you!

87:3

L: Listen, city of God,
  to the wonderful things he says about you;

1: *Of Zion it will be said*
  that all nations belong there,
  and the Most High will make her strong.

2: The Lord will write a list of the peoples,
  and include them all as citizens of Jerusalem.

U: *All who live there will sing and dance.*

89:1

L: Lord, I will always sing of your constant love;
   At all times I will proclaim your faithfulness.
   I know that your love will last forever,
   that Your faithfulness is as permanent as the sky.
1: How powerful you are!
   How great is your strength!
   Your kingdom is founded on righteousness and justice;
   Love and faithfulness are in all you do.
2: Happy are the people who worship you with songs,
   who live in the light of your kindness.
   Because of you they rejoice all day long
   and praise you because of your goodness.
L: Let us praise the Lord forever!
1: *Amen!*
2: Amen!

92:1

L: How good it is to give thanks to the Lord,
   to sing in your honor, Most High God,
   To proclaim your constant love every morning,
   and your faithfulness every night.
U: Your mighty acts, Lord, make me glad;
   because of what you have done I sing for joy.

96:1

L: Sing a new song to the Lord!
   Sing to the Lord, all the world!
U: Sing to the Lord, and praise him!
   Every day tell the good news that he has saved us!

96:7

L: All people on earth, praise the Lord!
1: *Praise his glory and might!*
2: Praise the Lord's glorious name;

1:   *bring an offering and come into his temple.*

2: Bow down before the Holy One when he appears;

U: *tremble before him, all the earth!*

98:1

L: Sing a new song to the Lord;
He has done wonderful things!
By his own power and holy strength,
he has won the victory.

1:   *The Lord announced his victory;*
he made his saving power known to the nations.
He kept his promise to the people of Israel,
with constant love and loyalty for them.
All people everywhere have seen the victory of our God!

2: Sing for joy to the Lord, all the earth;
praise him with songs and shouts of joy!

U: *Shout for joy before the Lord, the King!*

100

L: Sing for joy to the Lord, all the world!
Worship the Lord gladly,
and come before him with joyful songs!

1: Never forget that the Lord is God!
He made us, and we belong to him;
we are his people, we are his flock.

2: Enter his temple with thanksgiving,
go into his sanctuary with praise!
Give thanks to him and praise him!

U: The Lord is good;
his love lasts forever,
and his faithfulness for all time.

103:19

L: The Lord set up his throne in heaven;
he is king over all.

1: Praise the Lord, you strong and mighty angels,
who obey his commands, who listen to what he says!

2: *Praise the Lord, all you heavenly powers,*
you servants who do what he wants!
Praise the Lord, all his creatures;
in every place he rules!

U: *Praise the Lord, my soul!*

105:1

L: Give thanks to the Lord, proclaim his greatness,
and make known to the nations what he has done!

1: Sing to him, sing praise to him;
tell all the wonderful things he has done!

2: Be glad that we belong to him;
let all who serve the Lord rejoice!

106:47

L: Save us, Lord our God, and bring us back,
so that we may praise your holy name,
and be happy in thanking you.

U: Let us praise the Lord, the God of Israel;
Praise him now and forever!

L: All the people are to say, "Amen!"

U: *Amen! Praise the Lord!*

108:1

L: I am ready, God;

2: I am completely ready!
I will sing and praise you!

1: Wake up, my soul!
Wake up, my harp and lyre!
I will wake up the sun!

U: I will thank you among the nations, Lord!
I will praise you among the peoples!

113:1

L: Praise the Lord!

1: *You servants of the Lord, praise his name!*

2: His name will be praised, now and forever!

U: *From the east to the west,*
the Lord's name be praised!

114:7

L: Tremble, earth, at the Lord's coming,
at the presence of the God of Jacob,

U: *who changes rocks into pools of water,*
and stone cliffs into flowing springs.

116:12

L: What can I offer the Lord for all his goodness to me?

2: *I will bring an offering to the Lord,*
to thank him for saving me.
In the meeting of all his people,
I will give him what I have promised.

L: *I am your servant, Lord; you have set me free.*

1: I will give you a sacrifice of thanksgiving,
and offer my prayer to you.
In the meeting of all your people,
I will give you what I have promised.

U: Praise the Lord!

117

L: Praise the Lord, all nations!
Praise him, all peoples!

1: His constant love for us is strong,

2: and his faithfulness is eternal.

U: *Praise the Lord!*

118:1

L: Give thanks to the Lord, because he is good,
and his love is eternal.

1: *Let the people of Israel say, "His love is eternal."*

2: Let the priests of God say, "His love is eternal."

U: *Let all who fear him say, "His love is eternal."*

118:19

L: Open the gates of the temple for me;
I will go in and praise the Lord!

1: This is the gate of the Lord;
only the righteous can come in!

2: *I praise you, Lord, because you heard me,*
because you have given me victory!

1: The stone which the builders rejected as worthless,
turned out to be the most important of all.

2: *This was done by the Lord;*
what a wonderful sight it is!

L: What a wonderful day the Lord has given us;
let us be happy, let us celebrate!
Save us, Lord, save us!

U: God bless him who comes in the name of the Lord!

L: *From the temple of the Lord we bless you!*

1: The Lord is God;
he has been good to us.
With branches in your hands start the festival
and march around the altar.

2: *You are my God, and I give you thanks;*
I will proclaim your greatness.

U: *Give thanks to the Lord, because he is good,*
and his love is eternal.

121:1

L: I look to the mountains;
where will my help come from?

U: *My help comes from the Lord,*
who made heaven and earth.

122:1

L: I was glad when they said to me,
"Let us go to the Lord's house!"

1: *Now we are here,*
    standing inside the gates of Jerusalem!

2: This is where the tribes come, the tribes of Israel,
    to give thanks to the Lord.

1: *This is where the king judges his people.*

2: Pray for the peace of Jerusalem!

U: *May there be peace inside your walls.*

124

L: What if the Lord had not been on our side?
    Answer, Israel!

1: *"If the Lord had not been on our side,*
    then the flood would have carried us away,
    the water would have drowned us,
    the raging torrent would have drowned us."

2: Let us thank the Lord.
    We have escaped like a bird from the hunter's trap;
    the trap has been broken, and we are free!

U: *Our help comes from the Lord,*
    who made heaven and earth.

126

L: When the Lord brought us back to Zion,
    it was like a dream!
    How we laughed, how we sang for joy!

1: Then the other nations said about us,
    "The Lord did great things for them!"
    Indeed he did great things for us;
    how happy we were!

2: Lord, take us back to our land,
    just as your rain brings water back to dry riverbeds.
    Let those who cried while they planted,
    gather the harvest with joy!

1: Those who cried as they went out carrying the seed
    will come back singing for joy,
    bringing in the harvest!

127:1

L: If the Lord does not build the house,
the work of the builders is useless;

1: *if the Lord does not protect the city,*
it does no good for the sentries to stand guard.

2: It is useless to work so hard for a living,
getting up early and going to bed late;
the Lord gives rest to those he loves.

129:1

L: Israel, tell how cruelly your enemies have persecuted you
ever since you were young!

1: *"Ever since I was young,*
my enemies have persecuted me cruelly,
but they have not overcome me.

2: They cut deep wounds in my back,
and made it like a plowed field.
But the Lord, the righteous one,
has freed me from slavery."

134

L: Come, praise the Lord, all his servants,
all who serve in his temple at night.

1: *Raise your hands in prayer in the temple,*
and praise the Lord!

2: May the Lord, who made heaven and earth,
bless you from Zion.

U: *Praise the Lord!*

135:1

L: Praise the Lord!

1: *Praise his name, you servants of the Lord,*
who stand in the Lord's house,
in the sanctuary of our God.

2: Praise the Lord, because he is good;
sing praises to his name, because he is kind.

135:19

L: Praise the Lord, people of Israel;

1: *praise him, you priests of God!*

2: Praise the Lord, you Levites;

U: *praise him, all you that fear him!*

L: Praise the Lord in Zion, in Jerusalem, his home.

U: *Praise the Lord!*

136:1

L: Give thanks to the Lord, because he is good,

U: *and his love is eternal.*

1: Give thanks to the mightiest of all lords;

U: *his love is eternal.*

2: Give thanks to the God of heaven;

U: *his love is eternal.*

145:17

L: The Lord is righteous in all he does,
   merciful in all his acts.

2: *He is near to all who call to him,*
   who call to him with sincerity.

1: He supplies the needs of all who fear him;
   he hears their cry and saves them.

L: I will always praise the Lord;

U: *let all creatures praise his holy name forever!*

146:1

L: Praise the Lord!

U: *Praise the Lord, my soul!*

1: I will praise him as long as I live;
   I will sing to my God all my life.

2: The Lord will be king forever!
   Your God, Zion, will reign for all time!

U: *Praise the Lord!*

147:1

L: Praise the Lord!

1: *It is good to sing praise to our God;*
    it is pleasant and right to praise him.

2: Praise the Lord, Jerusalem!
    Praise your God, Zion!

1: He keeps your gates strong;
    he blesses your people.

2: Sing hymns of praise to the Lord;
    play music to our God.

148:1

L: Praise the Lord!

2: *Praise the Lord from heaven,*
    you that live in the heights above!

1: Praise him, sun and moon;
    praise him, shining stars!

2: *Praise him, young men and girls,*
    old people and children also!

L: Let them all praise the name of the Lord.

U: *His name is greater than all others;*
    his glory is above earth and heaven!

149:1

L: Praise the Lord!

1: Sing a new song to the Lord;
    praise him in the meeting of his faithful people!

2: Be glad, Israel, because of your creator;
    rejoice, people of Zion, because of your king!

1: Let God's people rejoice in their triumph,
    and sing joyfully at their feasts.

2: *Let them shout aloud as they praise God.*
    This is the victory of God's people!

U: *Praise the Lord!*

150:1

L: Praise the Lord!

1: Praise God in his temple!
   Praise his strength in heaven!

2: Praise him for the mighty things he has done!
   Praise his supreme greatness!

L: Praise the Lord, all living creatures!

U: *Praise the Lord!*

PSALMS OF PRAISE

3

L: I have so many enemies, Lord,
    so many who turn against me!

1:   *They talk about me and say,*
     "God will not help him!"

2: But you, Lord, always shield me from danger;
     you give me victory and restore my courage.
   I call to the Lord for help,
     from his sacred hill he answers me.

1: I lie down and sleep,
     I wake up safe, because the Lord protects me.
   I am not afraid of the thousands of enemies
   who surround me on every side.

U: *Come, Lord! Save me, my God!*

L: Salvation comes from the Lord —

U: *may he bless his people!*

5:1

L: Listen to my words, Lord, and hear my sighs.
     My king and my God, listen to my cry for help.

1: I will pray to you, Lord;
   in the morning you hear my voice;
     at sunrise I offer up my prayer,
     and wait for your answer.

2: You are not a God who is pleased with wrongdoing;
     you allow no evil in your presence.

1: As for me, I can come into your house,
   because of your great love;
     I can worship in your holy temple,
     and bow down to you in reverence.

2: Lord, lead me to do your will,
     and make your way plain for me to follow!

1: All who find safety in you will rejoice;
     they will always sing for joy.

2: You protect those who love you;
     because of you they are truly happy.

U: You bless those who obey you, Lord;
     your kindness protects them like a shield.

8

L: Lord, our Lord,
   your greatness is seen in all the world!

2:   *Your praise reaches up to the heavens;*
   it is sung by children and babies.
     You have built a fortress against your foes
     to stop your enemies and adversaries.

1: When I look at the sky, which you have made,
   at the moon and the stars, which you set in their places —
     what is man, that you think of him;
     mere man, that you care for him?

2: Yet you made him inferior only to yourself;
     you crowned him with glory and honor.
   You made him ruler over all you have made;
     you placed him over all things:
   sheep and cattle, and wild animals too;
   the birds and the fish,
   and all the creatures in the seas.

U: *Lord, our Lord,*
     your greatness is seen in all the world!

9:1

L: I will praise you, Lord, with all my heart,
     I will tell all the wonderful things you have done.

1: I will sing with joy because of you.
   I will sing praise to you, Most High!

2: The Lord is king forever;
   he has set up his throne for judgment.
   He rules the world with righteousness;
   he judges the people with justice.

1: The Lord is a refuge for the oppressed,
   a place of safety in times of trouble.
   Those who know you, Lord, will trust you;
   you do not abandon anyone who comes to you.

2: Sing praise to the Lord, who rules in Zion!
   Tell every nation what he has done!
   God remembers those who suffer;
   he does not forget their cry.

19

L: How clearly the sky reveals God's glory!
   How plainly it shows what he has done!

1: Each day announces it to the following day;
   each night repeats it to the next.
   No speech or words are used,
   no sound is heard;
   yet their voice goes out to all the world,
   their message reaches the ends of the earth.

2: God set up a tent in the sky for the sun;
   it comes out like a bridegroom striding from his house,
   like an athlete, eager to run a race.
   It starts at one end of the sky
   and goes around to the other.
   Nothing can hide from its heat.

U: *How clearly the sky reveals God's glory!*
   How plainly it shows what he has done!

22:22

L: I will tell my people what you have done;
   I will praise you in their meeting:

1: "Praise him, you servants of the Lord!
  Honor him, you descendants of Jacob;
  worship him, you people of Israel!
  He does not neglect the poor or ignore their suffering;
  he does not keep away from them,
  but answers when they call for help."

2: *In the full assembly I will praise you*
  for what you have done;
  in the presence of all who obey you
  I will offer the sacrifices I promised.
  The poor will eat as much as they want;
  those who come to the Lord will praise him.
  May they prosper forever!

1: All nations will remember the Lord;
  from every part of the world they will turn to him;
  all races will worship him.
  The Lord is king, and he rules over the nations.

2: All proud men will bow down to him;
  all mortal men will bow down before him,
  all those who are bound to die.
  Future generations will serve him;
  men will speak of the Lord to the coming generation.

U: *People not yet born will be told:*
  "The Lord saved his people!"

24

L: The world and all that is in it belong to the Lord;
  the earth and all who live on it are his.

U: He built it on the deep waters beneath the earth
  and laid its foundations in the ocean depths.

1: Who has the right to go up the Lord's hill?

2: *Who is allowed to enter his holy temple?*

L: He who is pure in act and in thought,
  who does not worship idols, or make false promises.

U: The Lord will bless him;
  God his Savior will declare him innocent.

L: Such are the people who come to God,
   who come into the presence of the God of Jacob.

1: Fling wide the gates,

2:   *open the ancient doors,*
     and the great king will come in!

L: Who is this great king?

U: *He is the Lord, strong and mighty,*
     the Lord, victorious in battle!

2: Fling wide the gates,

1:   *Open the ancient doors,*
     and the great king will come in!

L: Who is this great king?

U: *The Lord, he is the great king!*

29

L: Praise the Lord;
   praise his glory and power.

1: Praise the Lord's glorious name,
   bow down before the Holy One when he appears.

2: The Lord's voice is heard on the seas;
   the glorious God thunders,
   and his voice echoes over the ocean.
   The Lord's voice is heard
   in all its might and majesty!

1:   *The Lord's voice breaks the cedars,*
     even the cedars of Lebanon.
   He causes the mountains of Lebanon to jump like calves,
   and Mount Hermon to leap like a young bull.

2:   *The Lord's voice makes the lightning flash.*
     His voice makes the desert shake.

1: The Lord's voice makes the deer give birth,
   and leaves the trees stripped bare;
   in his temple all shout, "Glory to God!"

2: The Lord rules over the deep waters;
   he rules as king forever.

U: *The Lord gives strength to his people,*
    and blesses them with peace.

30

L: I praise you, Lord, because you have saved me
   and kept my enemies from gloating over me.
2: *I cried to you for help, Lord my God,*
    and you healed me.
   You brought me back from the world of the dead.
    I was with those who go down to the depths below,
    but you restored my life.

1: Sing praise to the Lord, his faithful people!
    Remember what the Holy One has done
    and give him thanks!

2: His anger lasts only a moment,
   his goodness is for a lifetime.
    There may be tears during the night,
    but joy comes in the morning.

1: I felt secure, and said to myself,
   "I will never be defeated."
    You are good to me, Lord;
    you have kept me safe as in a mountain fortress.

2: But when you hid yourself from me,
   I was filled with fear.
    I called to you, Lord; I begged for your help.
   What good will come from my death?
   What profit from my going to the grave?
    Hear me, Lord, and be merciful! Help me, Lord!

1: You have changed my sadness into a joyful dance;
    you have taken off my clothes of mourning,
    and given me clothes of joy.

2: So I will not be silent;
    I will sing praise to you.

U: Lord, you are my God,
    I will give thanks to you forever.

33

L: All you that are righteous,
   be glad because of what the Lord has done;
   praise him, all you that obey him!

1: Give thanks to the Lord with the harp,
   sing to him with stringed instruments.
   Sing a new song to him,
   play the harp with skill, and sing aloud!

2: The words of the Lord are true,
   and all his works are dependable.
   The Lord loves what is righteous and just;
   his constant love fills the earth.

1: The Lord created the heavens by his command,
   the sun, moon, and stars by his spoken word.
   He gathered all the seas into one place;
   he shut up the ocean depths in storerooms.

2: Fear the Lord, all the earth!
   Fear him, all people of the world!
   When he spoke, the world was created;
   at his command everything appeared.

1: The Lord frustrates the purposes of the nations;
   he keeps them from carrying out their plans.
   But his plans endure forever,
   his purposes last eternally.
   Happy is the nation whose God is the Lord;
   happy are the people he has chosen for his own!

2: The Lord looks down from heaven
   and sees all mankind.
   From where he rules he looks down
   on all who live on earth.
   He forms all their thoughts,
   and knows everything they do.

1: *A king does not win because of his powerful army;*
   a soldier does not triumph because of his strength.
   War horses are useless for victory;
   their great strength cannot save.

2: *The Lord watches over those who fear him,*
   those who trust in his constant love.
   He saves them from death;
   he keeps them alive in times of famine.

1: *We put our hope in the Lord;*
   he is our helper and protector.

2: We are glad because of him; we trust in his holy name.

U: *May your constant love be with us, Lord,*
   as we put our hope in you.

34

L: I will always thank the Lord;
   I will never stop praising him.

2: I will praise him for what he has done;
   may all who are oppressed listen and be glad!
   Proclaim with me the Lord's greatness;
   let us praise his name together!

1: I prayed to the Lord and he answered me;
   he freed me from all my fears.
   The oppressed look to him and are glad;
   they will never be disappointed.
   The helpless call to him, and he answers;
   he saves them from all their troubles.
   His angel guards those who fear the Lord
   and rescues them from danger.

2: Find out for yourself how good the Lord is!
   Happy is the man who finds safety with him!
   Fear the Lord, all his people;
   those who fear him have all they need.
   Even lions lack food and go hungry,
   but those who obey the Lord lack nothing good.

L: Come, my young friends, and listen to me,
   and I will teach you to fear the Lord.

1: *Would you like to enjoy life?*
   Do you want long life and happiness?

Then keep from speaking evil and from telling lies.
Turn away from evil and do good;
desire peace and do your best to have it.

2: The Lord watches over the righteous
and listens to their cries;
but he opposes those who do evil,
so that even their own people forget them.
Righteous men call to the Lord and he listens;
he rescues them from all their troubles.

1: The Lord is near to those who are discouraged;
he saves those who have lost all hope.
The good man suffers many troubles,
but the Lord saves him from them all;
the Lord preserves him completely;
not one of his bones is broken.

U: The Lord will save his servants;
those who go to him for protection will be spared.

40:1

L: I waited and waited for the Lord's help;
then he listened to me and heard my cry.

1: He pulled me out of a dangerous pit,
out of a muddy hole!
He set me safely on a rock and made me secure.

2: He taught me to sing a new song,
a song of praise to our God.
Many who see this will be afraid
and will put their trust in the Lord.

1: Happy is the person who trusts the Lord,
who does not turn to idols,
or join those who worship false gods.
You have done many things for us, Lord my God;
there is no one like you!
You have made so many wonderful plans for us.
If I tried to speak of all of them,
there would be more than I could tell.

2: You do not want sacrifices and offerings;
you do not ask for animals
burned whole on the altar,
or sacrifices to take away sins.
Instead you have given me ears to hear you,
and so I answered, "Here I am;
your instructions for me
are in the book of the Law.
How I love to do your will, my God!
I keep your teaching in my heart."

1: In the meeting of all your people, Lord,
I told the good news that you save.
You know that I will never stop telling it.
I have not kept the news of salvation to myself;
I have always spoken
of your faithfulness and help.
In the meeting of all your people
I have not been silent
about your constant love and loyalty.

U: *Lord, I know you will never stop*
being merciful to me!
Your love and loyalty will always keep me safe.

42

L: As a deer longs for a stream of cool water,
so I long for you, God.

1: *I thirst for you, the living God;*
when can I go and worship in your presence?
Day and night I cry, and tears are my only food;
all the time my enemies ask me, "Where is your God?"

2: My heart breaks when I remember the past,
when I went with the crowds to the house of God,
and led them as they walked along,
a happy crowd, singing and shouting praise to God.

1: Why am I so sad? Why am I troubled?
I will put my hope in God,

and once again I will praise him,
my Savior and my God.

2: My heart is breaking, so I will remember him;
  in my exile in the region of the Jordan
  I will remember him.

1: The ocean depths call out to each other,
  and the waterfalls of God are roaring!
  They are like the waves of sorrow
  with which he floods my soul.

2: May the Lord show his constant love every day!
  May I sing praise to him every night,
  and pray to God, who gives me life.

1: Why am I so sad?

2: Why am I troubled?

U: *I will put my hope in God,*
  and once again I will praise him,
  my Savior and my God.

43:3

L: Send your light and your truth;
  may they lead me
  and bring me back to Zion, your sacred hill,
  and to your temple, where you live!

1: Then I will go to your altar, God,
  because you give me joy and happiness;

2: *I will play my harp and sing praise to you, God, my God!*

1: Why am I so sad?

2: *Why am I so troubled?*

U: I will put my hope in God,
  and once again I will praise him, my Savior and my God.

46

L: God is our shelter and strength,
  always ready to help in times of trouble.

1:   *So we will not be afraid, even if the earth is shaken*
     and mountains fall into the ocean depths;
     even if the seas roar and rage,
     and the hills are shaken by the violence.

2:   *There is a river that brings joy to the city of God,*
     to the sacred house of the Most High.

1: God lives in the city, and it will never be destroyed;
     at early dawn he will come to its help.
   Nations are terrified, kingdoms are shaken;
     God roars out, and the earth dissolves.

U: The Lord Almighty is with us;
     the God of Jacob is our refuge!

2: Come, see what the Lord has done!
     See what amazing things he has done on earth!
   He stops wars all over the world;
     he breaks bows, destroys spears,
     and sets shields on fire!

   He says, "Stop your fighting, and know that I am God,
   supreme among the nations, supreme over the world!"

U: *The Lord Almighty is with us;*
     the God of Jacob is our refuge!

48

L: The Lord is great, and must be highly praised
   in the city of our God, on his sacred mountain.

1:   *Zion, the mountain of God, is high and beautiful;*
   the city of the great king brings joy to all the world!
     God has shown that there is safety with him
     inside the fortresses of the city.

2: We have heard about what God has done,
   and now we have seen it
   in the city of our God, the Lord Almighty;
     he will keep the city safe forever.

1: Inside your temple, God,
     we think of your constant love.

You are praised by people everywhere,
and your fame extends over all the earth.

2: You rule with justice;
   let the people of Zion be glad!
   You give right judgments;
   let there be joy in the cities of Judah!

1: Walk all around Mount Zion and count its towers,
   take notice of its walls, and examine its fortresses,
   so that you may tell the next generation
   that this God is our God, forever and ever;

U: *he will lead us for all time to come.*

57

L: Be merciful to me, God, be merciful,
   because I come to you for safety.

1: *In the shadow of your wings I find protection,*
   until all danger is past.
   I call to God, the Most High,
   to God, who supplies all my needs.

2: *He will answer from heaven and save me;*
   he will defeat my attackers.
   God will show me his constant love and faithfulness.

U: *God, show your greatness in the sky,*
   and your glory over all the earth!

L: I am ready, God; I am completely ready!
   I will sing and praise you!

1: Wake up, my soul!
   Wake up, my harp and lyre!
   I will wake up the sun!

2: I will thank you among the nations, Lord!
   I will praise you among the peoples!

1: Your constant love reaches up to heaven,
   your faithfulness to the skies.

U: *God, show your greatness in the sky,*
   and your glory over all the earth!

63:1

L: God, you are my God,
  I long for you.

1: My whole being desires you;
  my soul is thirsty for you,
  like a dry, worn-out, and waterless land.

2: Let me see you in the sanctuary;
  let me see how mighty and glorious you are.

1: Your constant love is better than life itself,
  and so I will praise you.
  I will give thanks to you as long as I live;
  I will raise my hands to you in prayer.
  My soul will feast and be satisfied,
  and I will sing glad songs of praise to you.

2: As I lie in bed I remember you;
  all night long I think of you,
  because you have always been my help.
  In the shadow of your wings I sing for joy.

U: *I cling to you, and your hand keeps me safe.*

65

L: God, people must praise you in Zion
  and give you what they have promised,
  because you answer prayers.

1: All men shall come to you on account of their sins.
  Our faults defeat us, but you forgive them.
  Happy are those whom you choose,
  whom you bring to live in your sanctuary!
  We shall be satisfied
  with the good things of your house,
  the blessings of your sacred temple!

2: You answer us, God our Savior,
  and you save us by doing wonderful things.
  People all over the world,
  and across the distant seas, trust in you.

1: You set the mountains in place by your strength,
   showing your mighty power.
   You calm the roar of the seas
   and the noise of the waves;
   you calm the uproar of the peoples.

2: The whole world is afraid,
   because of the great things that you have done.
   Your actions bring shouts of joy
   from one end of the earth to the other.

1: You show your care for the land by sending rain;
   you make it rich and fertile.
   The streams you have given never run dry;
   they provide the earth with crops—
   this is what you have done.

2: You send abundant rain on the plowed fields
   and soak them with water;
   you soften the soil with showers
   and cause the young plants to grow.

1: What a rich harvest your goodness provides!
   Wherever you go there is plenty!

2: The pastures are filled with flocks;
   the hillsides are full of joy.

U: The fields are covered with sheep;
   the valleys are full of wheat;
   they shout and sing for joy!

66

L: Praise God with shouts of joy, all people!

U: *Sing to the glory of his name;*
   offer him glorious praise!

1: Say to God, "How wonderful are the things you do!
   Your power is so great
   that your enemies bow in fear before you.
   Everyone on earth worships you; they sing praises to you,
   they sing praises to your name."

2: Come and see what God has done,
his wonderful acts among men.
He changed the sea into dry land;
our ancestors crossed the river on foot.
There we rejoiced because of what he had done.
He rules forever by his might
and keeps his eyes on the nations.
Let no rebels rise against him!

1: Praise our God, all nations;
let your praise be heard.
He has kept us alive and has not allowed us to fall.
You have put us to the test, God;
as silver is purified by fire, so you have tested us.

2: You let us fall into a trap
and placed heavy burdens on our backs.
You let our enemies trample us;
we went through fire and flood,
but now you have brought us to a place of safety.

1: I will bring burnt offerings to your house;
I will offer you what I promised.
I will give you what I said I would,
when I was in trouble.

2: *Come and listen, all who honor God,*
and I will tell you what he has done for me.
I cried to him for help;
I was ready to praise him with songs.
If I had ignored my sins,
the Lord would not have listened to me.
But God has indeed heard me;
he has listened to my prayer.

U: *I praise God, because he did not reject my*
prayer
or keep back his constant love from me.

67:1

L: God, be merciful to us and bless us;

U:　*look on us with kindness,*
　　that the whole world may know your will;
　　that all nations may know your salvation.

1: May the peoples praise you, God;

2:　*may all peoples praise you!*

1: May the nations be glad and sing for joy,
　because you judge the peoples with justice
　and guide all the nations.

2:　*May the peoples praise you, God;*

1:　*may all peoples praise you!*

2: God, our God, has blessed us.

U:　*God has blessed us;*
　　may all people everywhere honor him.

68:16

L: Why do you, from your mighty peaks, look with scorn
　on the mountain that God chose to live on?

U:　*The Lord will live there forever!*

1: With his many thousands of mighty chariots,
　the Lord comes from Sinai into the holy place.

2:　*He goes up to the heights,*
　　taking many captives with him;
　he receives gifts from rebellious men.

U:　*The Lord God will live there.*

71

L: Lord, I am safe with you;
　　never let me be defeated!

2: Because you are righteous, help me and rescue me.
　　Listen to me and save me!
　Be my secure shelter,
　and a strong fortress to protect me;
　　you are my refuge and defense.

1: Lord, I put my hope in you;
   I have trusted in you since I was young.
   I have relied on you all my life;
   you have protected me since I was born;
   I will always praise you!

2: My life has been a mystery to many,
   but you are my strong defender.
   All day long I praise you and proclaim your glory.

1: I will always put my hope in you;
   I will praise you more and more.
   I will tell of your righteousness;
   all day long I will speak of your salvation,
   though it is more than I can understand.

2: I will praise your power, Lord God;
   I will proclaim your righteousness, yours alone.

1: Be with me while I proclaim your power and might
   to all generations to come.

2: *Your righteousness, God, reaches the skies.*
   You have done great things;
   there is no one like you!
   You have sent troubles and suffering on me,
   but you will restore my strength;
   you will keep me from the grave.
   You will make me greater than ever;
   you will comfort me again.

1: I will indeed praise you;
   I will praise your faithfulness, my God.

2: I will play hymns to you, the Holy One of Israel.
   I will shout for joy as I play for you.

U: *With my whole being I will sing,*
   because you have saved me.

81

L: Shout with joy to God our defender;
   sing praises to the God of Jacob!

1: Start the music and play the tambourines;

play pleasant music on the harps and the lyres.
Blow the horn for the festival;
when the moon is new, and when the moon is full.

2:   *This is the law in Israel,*
     an order from the God of Jacob.
   He commanded it to the people of Israel,
   when he marched out against the land of Egypt.

1:   *I hear an unfamiliar voice saying,*
     "I took the heavy loads off your backs;
     I let you put down your workbaskets.
   When you were in trouble you called to me,
   and I saved you.
     From my hiding place in the storm, I answered you.

2: "Listen, my people, to my warning;
   Israel, how I wish you would listen to me!
     You must never serve a foreign god,
     or worship anyone else but me.
   I am the Lord, your God,
   who brought you out of the land of Egypt.
     Open your mouth, and I will feed you.

1: "But my people would not listen to me;
   Israel would not obey me.
     So I let them go their stubborn ways
     and do whatever they wanted.

2: "How I wish my people would listen to me;
   how I wish they would obey me!

U: *"I would feed you with the finest wheat*
     and satisfy you with wild honey."

84

L: How I love your temple, Almighty God!
    How I want to be there!

2: I long for the courts of the Lord's temple.
    With my whole being I sing with joy to the living God.

1: Even the sparrows have built a nest,
   and the swallows have their own home;

they keep their young near your altars,
Lord Almighty, my king and my God.

U: *How happy are those who live in your temple,*
always singing praise to you!

2: How happy are those whose strength comes from you,
who are eager to make the pilgrimage to Mount Zion.

1: *As they pass through the dry valley*
it becomes a place of springs;
the early rain fills it with pools.
They grow stronger as they go;
they will see the God of gods on Zion!

U: Hear my prayer, Lord God Almighty; listen, God of Jacob!

2: *One day spent in your temple*
is better than a thousand anywhere else;
I would rather stand at the gate of the house of my God
than live in the homes of the wicked.

1: *The Lord is our protector and glorious king,*
blessing us with kindness and honor.
He does not refuse any good thing
to those who do what is right.

U: *Happy are those who trust in you, Almighty God!*

89:1

L: Lord, I will always sing of your constant love;
at all times I will proclaim your faithfulness.

1: I know that your love will last forever,
that your faithfulness is as permanent as the sky.
You said, "I have made a covenant with the man I chose;
I have promised my servant David,
'A descendant of yours will always be king;
I will preserve your kingdom forever.'"

2: The gods in heaven sing of the wonderful things you do;
they sing of your faithfulness, Lord.
No one in heaven is like you, Lord;
none of the gods is your equal.

You are respected in the council of the gods,
and greatly feared by all around you.

1:   *Lord God Almighty, none is as mighty as you;*
     in all things you are faithful, Lord.
     You rule over the powerful sea;
       you calm its angry waves.
     You crushed the monster and killed it;
       with your mighty strength you defeated your enemies.

2:   The earth is yours, and heaven also;
       you created the world and everything in it;
     you made the north and the south;
     Mount Tabor and Mount Hermon sing to you for joy.

     How powerful you are! How great is your strength!
     Your kingdom is founded on righteousness and justice;
       love and faithfulness are in all you do.

:   Happy are the people who worship you with songs,
     who live in the light of your kindness.
       Because of you they rejoice all day long
       and praise you because of your goodness.

:   Let us praise the Lord forever!

J: *Amen! Amen!*

92

L: How good it is to give thanks to the Lord,
     to sing in your honor, Most High God,
       to proclaim your constant love every morning,
       and your faithfulness every night.

1:   Your mighty acts, Lord, make me glad;
       because of what you have done I sing for joy.

2:   How great are your acts, Lord!
       How deep are your thoughts!
     Here is something a fool cannot know,
     a stupid man cannot understand:
       the wicked may grow like weeds,
       and all evildoers may prosper;

> *yet they will be totally destroyed,*
> *because you, Lord, are supreme forever.*

1: The righteous will flourish like palm trees;
   they will grow like the cedars of Lebanon.
   They are like trees planted in the house of the Lord,
   that flourish in the temple of our God,
   that still bear fruit in old age,
   and are always green and strong.

U: *This shows that the Lord is just;*
    in him, my defender, there is no wrong.

93

L: The Lord is king!

1: *He is clothed with majesty, and covered with strength.*
    Surely the earth is set firmly in place
    and cannot be moved.
       Your throne, Lord, has been firm from the beginning,
       and you existed before time began.
2: The ocean depths raise their voice, Lord;
   they raise their voice and roar.
      The Lord rules supreme in heaven,
      greater than the roar of the ocean,
      more powerful than the waves of the sea.

U: Your laws are eternal, Lord,
      your temple is holy indeed, forever and ever.

95:1

L: Come, let us praise the Lord!
      Let us sing for joy to our protector and Savior!

1: Let us come before him with thanksgiving,
      and sing joyful songs of praise!

2: For the Lord is a mighty God,
   a mighty king over all the gods.
      He rules over the whole earth,
      from the deepest caves to the highest hills.

1: He rules over the sea, which he made;
   the land also, which he himself formed.

2: *Come, let us bow down and worship him;*
let us kneel before the Lord, our Maker!

U: He is our God;
we are the people he looks after,
the flock for which he provides.

96

L: Sing a new song to the Lord!

U: *Sing to the Lord, all the world!*
Sing to the Lord, and praise him!
Every day tell the good news that he has saved us!

 : Proclaim his glory to the nations,
his mighty acts to all peoples.

2: *The Lord is great, and must be highly praised;*
he must be feared more than all the gods.

1: The gods of all other nations are only idols,
but the Lord made the heavens.

2: *Glory and majesty are around him,*
greatness and beauty are in his temple.

1: All people on earth, praise the Lord!
Praise his glory and might!

2: Praise the Lord's glorious name;
bring an offering and come into his temple.

L: Bow down before the Holy One when he appears;

U: *Tremble before him, all the earth!*

1: Say to all the nations, "The Lord is king!
The earth is set firmly in place and cannot be moved;
he will judge all peoples with justice."

2: Be glad, earth and sky!
Roar, sea, and all the creatures in you;
be glad, fields, and everything in you!
Then the trees in the woods will shout for joy
before the Lord, because he comes to rule the earth.

U: *He will rule all peoples of the world*
with justice and fairness.

97

L: The Lord is king! Be glad, earth!
Rejoice, all you islands of the seas!

1: Clouds and darkness are around him;
his kingdom is based on righteousness and justice.
Fire goes in front of him,
and burns up his enemies around him.
His lightning lights up the world;
the earth sees it and trembles.
The hills melt like wax before the Lord,
before the Lord of all the earth.
The heavens proclaim his righteousness,
and all peoples see his glory.

2: All who worship images are ashamed,
all who boast of their idols;
all the gods bow down before him.
The people of Zion are glad,
and the cities of Judah rejoice,
because of your judgments, Lord!
Lord Almighty, you are ruler of all the earth;
you are much greater than all the gods.

1: Hate evil, you who love the Lord.
He protects the lives of his people,
he rescues them from the power of the wicked.
Light shines on the righteous, and gladness on the good.

2: *All you that are righteous,*
be glad, because of what the Lord has done!
Remember what the Holy One has done,
and give thanks to him!

98

L: Sing a new song to the Lord;
he has done wonderful things!
By his own power and holy strength,
he has won the victory.

1: *The Lord announced his victory;*
he made his saving power known to the nations.

2: He kept his promise to the people of Israel,
with constant love and loyalty for them.

1: *All people everywhere have seen the victory of our God!*

2: Sing for joy to the Lord, all the earth;
praise him with songs and shouts of joy!

1: Sing praises to the Lord with harps;
play music on the harps!

2: *With trumpets and horns,*
shout for joy before the Lord, the king!

1: Roar, sea, and all creatures in you;
sing, earth, and all who live there!

2: Clap your hands, oceans;
hills, sing together with joy before the Lord,
because he comes to rule the earth!

U: He will rule all peoples of the world
with justice and fairness.
Sing for joy to the Lord!

99

L: The Lord is king;
the people tremble;

2: He sits on his throne on the cherubim;
the earth shakes.

1: The Lord is mighty in Zion;
he rules over all the nations.

2: Everyone will praise his great and majestic name.
Holy is he!

1: Mighty king, you love what is right;
you have brought justice to Israel;
you have brought righteousness and fairness.

2: Praise the Lord our God; worship before his throne!
Holy is he!

1: Moses and Aaron were his priests,
and Samuel was one who worshiped him;
they called to the Lord and he answered them.

2: He spoke to them from the column of cloud;
   they obeyed the laws and commandments
   that he gave them.

L: Lord, our God, you answered your people;

U: *you showed them that you are a God who forgives.*

L: Praise the Lord our God;

U: *The Lord our God is holy!*

100

L: Sing for joy to the Lord, all the world!
   Worship the Lord gladly,
   and come before him with joyful songs!

1: Never forget that the Lord is God!
   He made us, and we belong to him;
   we are his people, we are his flock.

2: Enter his temple with thanksgiving,
   go into his sanctuary with praise!
   Give thanks to him and praise him!

U: The Lord is good;
   his love lasts forever,
   and his faithfulness for all time.

103

L: Praise the Lord, my soul!

1: *All my being, praise his holy name!*
   Praise the Lord, my soul,
   and do not forget how kind he is.
   He forgives all my sins and heals all my diseases;
   he saves me from the grave
   and blesses me with love and mercy;
   he fills my life with good things,
   so that I stay young and strong like an eagle.

2: The Lord judges in favor of the oppressed
   and gives them their rights.
   He told his plans to Moses
   and let the people of Israel see his mighty acts.

L: *The Lord is merciful and loving,*
    slow to become angry, and full of constant love.

1: He does not keep on reprimanding;
    he is not angry forever.
    He does not punish us as we deserve,
    or repay us for our sins and wrongs.

2: As high as the sky is above the earth,
    so great is his love for those who fear him.
    As far as the east is from the west,
    so far does he remove our sins from us.

1: As kind as a father is to his children,
    so the Lord is kind to those who fear him.
    He knows what we are made of; ·
    he remembers that we are dust.
    As for man, his life is like grass;
    he grows and flourishes like a wild flower.
    Then the wind blows on it, and it is gone,
    and no one sees it again.

2: *But the Lord's love for those who honor him*
    lasts forever,
    and his goodness endures for all generations,
    to those who are true to his covenant,
    and who faithfully obey his commandments.

L: The Lord set up his throne in heaven;
    he is king over all.

1: Praise the Lord, you strong and mighty angels,
    who obey his commands, who listen to what he says!

2: *Praise the Lord, all you heavenly powers,*
    you servants who do what he wants!
    Praise the Lord, all his creatures;
    in every place he rules!

U: *Praise the Lord, my soul!*

104

L: Praise the Lord, my soul!

1: *Lord, my God, how great you are!*

You are clothed with majesty and glory;
you cover yourself with light.
You stretched out the heavens like a tent,
and built your home on the waters above.

2: *You use the clouds as your chariot,*
    and walk on the wings of the wind.
You use the winds as your messengers,
and flashes of lightning as your servants.

1: *You make springs flow in the valleys,*
    and water run between the hills.
They provide water for the wild animals;
the wild donkeys quench their thirst;
    in the trees near by
    the birds make their nests and sing.

2: From heaven you send rain on the mountains,
and the earth is filled with your blessings.
    You make grass grow for the cattle,
    and plants for man to use,
so he can grow his crops,
and produce wine to make him happy,
olive oil to make him cheerful,
and bread to give him strength.

1: *You created the moon to mark the months;*
    the sun knows the time to set.
You made the night, and in the darkness
all the wild animals come out.
    The young lions roar while they hunt,
    looking for the food that God gives them.

2: When the sun rises they go back
and lie down in their dens.
    Then men go out to do their work,
    and keep working until evening.

1: Lord, you have made so many things!
    How wisely you made them all!
    The earth is filled with your creatures.
There is the ocean, large and wide,

where countless creatures live,
large and small alike;

2: *All of them depend on you,*
to give them food when they need it.
You give it to them, and they eat it;
you provide food, and they are satisfied.

1: When you turn away, they are afraid;
when you hold back your breath, they die,
and go back to the soil they came from.
But when you give them breath, they live;
you give new life to the earth.

2: May the glory of the Lord last forever!
May the Lord be happy with what he made!
He looks at the earth, and it trembles;
he touches the mountains, and they pour out smoke.

1: I will sing to the Lord all my life;
I will sing praises to my God as long as I live.

2: May he be pleased with my song,
because he makes me glad.

1: *Praise the Lord, my soul!*

2: *Praise the Lord!*

107:1

L: Give thanks to the Lord, because he is good;
his love is eternal!

1: Join me in praising the Lord,
all you whom he has saved.
He has rescued you from your enemies,
and brought you back from foreign countries,
from east and west, from north and south.

2: Some wandered in the trackless desert,
and could not find their way to a city to live in;
they were hungry and thirsty,
and had given up all hope.

1: In their trouble they called to the Lord,

and he saved them from their distress.
He led them out, straight to a city to live in.

2: They must thank the Lord for his constant love,
for the wonderful things he did for them!
*He satisfies those who are thirsty,
and the hungry he fills with good things.*

108:1

L: I am ready, God; I am completely ready!
I will sing and praise you!

1: Wake up, my soul! Wake up, my harp and lyre!
I will wake up the sun!

2: I will thank you among the nations, Lord!
I will praise you among the peoples!

1: Your constant love reaches above the heavens,
your faithfulness to the skies.

2: *God, show your greatness in the sky,
and your glory over all the earth!*

U: Save us by your might; answer my prayer,
so that the people you love may be rescued.

111

L: Praise the Lord!

1: *With all my heart I will thank the Lord,
in the meeting of his people.*
How wonderful are the things the Lord does!
All who are pleased with them want to understand them.
*All he does is full of honor and majesty;
his righteousness is eternal.*

2: The Lord does not let us forget his wonderful actions;
he is kind and merciful.
He provides food for those who fear him;
he never forgets his covenant.
He has shown his power to his people.

1: *In all he does he is faithful and just;
all his commandments are dependable.*

They last for all time;
they were given in truth and righteousness.

2: He brought salvation to his people,
and made an eternal covenant with them.
Holy and mighty is he!

1: The way to become wise is to fear the Lord;
he gives sound judgment to all who obey his commands.

2: *He is to be praised forever!*
Praise the Lord!

113

L: Praise the Lord!

1: *Servants of the Lord, praise his name!*
2: His name will be praised, now and forever!

U: *From the east to the west,*
the Lord's name be praised!

L: The Lord rules over all nations,
his glory is above the heavens.

1: There is no one like the Lord our God;
he lives in the heights above,
but he bends down to see the heavens and the earth.

2: He raises the poor from the dust;
he lifts the needy from their misery,
and makes them companions of princes,
the princes of his people.

L: Praise the Lord!

U: *Praise the Lord!*

115

L: To you alone, Lord,
to you alone, and not to us, must glory be given,
because of your constant love and faithfulness.

1: Why should the nations ask us, "Where is your God?"

2:   *Our God is in heaven, doing whatever he wishes.*

1: Their gods are made of silver and gold,
formed by human hands.
     They have mouths, but cannot speak,
     and eyes, but cannot see.
They have ears, but cannot hear,
and noses, but cannot smell.

2:   *They have hands, but cannot feel,*
     and feet, but cannot walk;
     they cannot make a sound.

L: Trust in the Lord, people of Israel!
He helps you and protects you.

1:   *Trust in the Lord, you priests of God!*
     He helps you and protects you.

2: Trust in the Lord, all who fear him!
He helps you and protects you.

1:   *The Lord remembers us and will bless us;*
     he will bless the people of Israel,
     and all the priests of God.

2: He will bless all who fear him,
the great and the small alike.

L: *May you be blessed by the Lord,*
     who made heaven and earth!

U: We, the living, will give thanks to him,
now and forever.
     Praise the Lord!

116

L: I love the Lord, because he hears me;
he listens to my prayers.
     He listens to me every time I call to him.

1: Death drew its ropes tight around me,
the horrors of the grave closed in on me;
I was filled with fear and anxiety.
     Then I called to the Lord, "I beg you, Lord, save me!"

2: The Lord is merciful and good;
   our God is compassionate.
   The Lord protects the helpless;
   when I was in danger, he saved me.
   Be confident, my heart,
   because the Lord has been good to me.

1: *The Lord has saved me from death;*
   he stopped my tears and kept me from defeat.
   And so I walk in the presence of the Lord
   in the world of the living.

2: *I kept on believing, even when I said,*
   "I am completely crushed,"
   even when I was afraid and said,
   "No one can be trusted."

L: What can I offer the Lord for all his goodness
   to me?

2: *I will bring an offering to the Lord,*
   to thank him for saving me.
   In the meeting of all his people,
   I will give him what I have promised.

L: *I am your servant, Lord; you have set me free.*

1: I will give you a sacrifice of thanksgiving,
   and offer my prayer to you.
   In the meeting of all your people,
   I will give you what I have promised.

U: *Praise the Lord!*

119:89

L: Your word, Lord, will last forever;
   it is firm in heaven.

1: *Your faithfulness endures through all the ages;*
   you have set the earth in place and it remains.

2: *All things remain to this day because of your command,*
   because they are all your servants.

1: If your law had not been the source of my joy,
   I would have died from my punishment.

2: *I am yours — save me! I have tried to obey your commands.*

1: Wicked men are waiting to kill me,
but I will meditate on your laws.

2: *I have learned that nothing is perfect;
but your commandment has no limits.*

L: Your word, Lord, will last forever;

U: *Your faithfulness endures through all the ages.*

132

L: Lord, do not forget David and all the work he did.

1: *Remember, Lord, what he promised,
the vow he made to you, the mighty God of Israel:*
"I will not go home or go to bed; I will not rest or sleep,
until I provide a place for the Lord,
a home for the Mighty God of Israel."

2: *We heard about the covenant box in Bethlehem,
and found it in the fields.*
"Let us go to the Lord's house;
let us worship before his throne!"

1: May the priests proclaim that you save your people;
may all your people shout for joy!

2: You made a promise to your servant David,
and you will not take it back:
*"I will make one of your sons king,
and he will rule after you."*

1: The Lord has chosen Zion;
he wants to make his home there:
*"This is where I will live forever;
this is where I want to rule.*
I will richly provide Zion with all she needs;
I will satisfy her poor with food.

2: *"I will have her priests proclaim that I save,
and her people will sing and shout for joy.*
Here I will make one of David's descendants a great king;

here I will preserve the rule of my chosen king.

U: "I will cover his enemies with shame,
    but his kingdom will prosper and flourish."

135

L: Praise the Lord!

1:    *Praise his name, you servants of the Lord,*
    who stand in the Lord's house,
    in the sanctuary of our God.
    Praise the Lord, because he is good;
    sing praises to his name, because he is kind.
    He chose Jacob for himself,
    the people of Israel for his own.
2:    *I know that our Lord is great;*
    he is greater than all the gods.
    He does whatever he wishes in heaven and on earth,
    in the seas and in the depths below.
    He brings storm clouds from the ends of the earth;
    he makes lightning for the storms,
    and brings out the wind from his storeroom.

1: Lord, men will always know that you are God;
    all generations will remember you.
    The Lord will take pity on his people;
    he will set his servants free.

2: The idols of the nations are made of silver and gold;
    they are formed by human hands.
    They have mouths, but cannot speak,
    and eyes, but cannot see.
    They have ears, but cannot hear;
    there is no breath in their mouths.

L: Praise the Lord, people of Israel;

1:    *praise him, you priests of God!*

2: Praise the Lord, you Levites;

U: *praise him, all you that fear him!*

L: Praise the Lord in Zion, in Jerusalem, his home.

U: *Praise the Lord!*

136

L: Give thanks to the Lord, because he is good;
U: *his love is eternal.*
 1: Give thanks to the greatest of all gods;
U: *his love is eternal.*
 2: Give thanks to the mightiest of all lords;
U: *his love is eternal.*
 1: He alone does great miracles;
U: *his love is eternal.*
 2: By his wisdom he made the heavens;
U: *his love is eternal.*
 1: He built the earth on the deep waters;
U: *his love is eternal.*
 2: He made the sun and the moon;
   the sun to rule over the day,
   the moon and the stars to rule over the night;
U: *his love is eternal.*

 1: He led the people of Israel out of Egypt
   with his strong hand, his powerful arm;
U: *his love is eternal.*
 2: He divided the Sea of Reeds;
   he led his people through it;
U: *his love is eternal;*
 1: He led his people in the desert;
U: *his love is eternal.*
 2: He did not forget us when we were defeated;
U: *his love is eternal;*
 1: he freed us from our enemies;
U: *his love is eternal.*
 2: He gives food to all men and animals;

U: *his love is eternal.*

L: Give thanks to the God of heaven;

U: *his love is eternal.*

137:1

L: By the rivers of Babylon
we sat and cried when we remembered Zion.

1:   *On the willows nearby we hung our harps.*
Those who captured us told us to sing;
they told us to entertain them:
"Sing us a song about Zion!"

2:   *How can we sing the Lord's song in a foreign land?*
May I never be able to play the harp again,
if I forget you, Jerusalem!

U: *May I never be able to sing again,*
if I do not remember you,
if I do not think of you as my greatest joy!

138

L: I thank you, Lord, with all my heart;
I sing praise to you before the gods.

1: I bow down and praise your name,
because of your constant love and faithfulness,
because you have shown that you and your commands
are supreme.
You answered me when I called to you;
with your strength you strengthened me.

2: All the kings of the earth will praise you, Lord,
because they have heard your promises.
They will sing about what the Lord has done,
and about his great glory.

1: Even though the Lord is so high above,
he cares for the lowly,
and the proud cannot hide from him.

2:   *Even when I am surrounded by troubles,*
you keep me safe;

You will do everything you have promised me;

U: *Lord, your love is constant forever.*
      complete the work that you have begun.

145:1

L: I will proclaim your greatness, my God and king;
   I will thank you forever and ever.

1: Every day I will thank you;
   I will praise you forever and ever.
   The Lord is great, and must be highly praised;
   His greatness is beyond understanding.

2: What you have done will be praised
   from one generation to the next;
   they will proclaim your mighty acts.
   Men will speak of your glory and majesty,
   and I will meditate on your wonderful deeds.
   Men will speak of your mighty acts,
   and I will proclaim your greatness.
   They will tell about all your goodness,
   and sing about your kindness.

1: *The Lord is loving and merciful,*
   slow to become angry and full of constant love.
   He is good to everyone
   and has compassion on all he made.

2: *All your creatures, Lord, will praise you,*
   and your people will give you thanks!
   They will speak of the glory of your kingdom
   and tell of your might,
   so that all men will know your mighty acts
   and the glorious majesty of your kingdom.

U: *Your kingdom is eternal, and you are king forever.*

145:13

L: God is faithful to his promises,
   and good in all he does.

1: *He helps all who are in trouble;*

he raises all who are humbled.
All living things look hopefully to him,
and he gives them food when they need it.
He gives them enough and satisfies the needs of all.

2: The Lord is righteous in all he does,
merciful in all his acts.
He is near to all who call to him,
who call to him with sincerity.
He supplies the needs of all who fear him;
he hears their cry and saves them.

L: I will always praise the Lord;

U: *let all creatures praise his holy name forever!*

146

L: Praise the Lord!

U: *Praise the Lord, my soul!*

1: I will praise him as long as I live;
I will sing to my God all my life.

2: Don't put your trust in human leaders,
or anyone else who cannot save you.
When they die they return to the soil;
on that day all their plans come to an end.

1: Happy is the man who has the God of Jacob to help him,
and depends on the Lord his God,
who created heaven, earth, and sea,
and all that is in them.
He always keeps his promises;
he judges in favor of the oppressed
and gives food to the hungry.

2: The Lord sets prisoners free
and gives sight to the blind.
He raises all who are humbled;
he loves his righteous people.
He protects the foreigners who live in the land;
he helps widows and orphans,
but ruins the plans of the wicked.

L: The Lord will be king forever!
Your God, Zion, will reign for all time!

U: *Praise the Lord!*

147:1

L: Praise the Lord!

1: *It is good to sing praise to our God;*
it is pleasant and right to praise him.
The Lord is restoring Jerusalem;
he is bringing back the exiles.
He heals the brokenhearted,
and bandages their wounds.

2: He has determined the number of the stars
and calls each one by name.
Great and almighty is our Lord;
his knowledge cannot be measured.

He raises the humble,
but crushes the wicked to the ground.

1: *Sing hymns of praise to the Lord;*
play music to our God.
He spreads clouds over the sky;
he provides rain for the earth,
and makes grass grow on the hills.
He gives animals their food,
and feeds the young ravens when they call.

2: His pleasure is not in strong horses,
nor his delight in brave soldiers;
but he takes pleasure in those who fear him,
in those who trust in his constant love.

147:12

L: Praise the Lord, Jerusalem!

1: *Praise your God, Zion!*
He keeps your gates strong;
he blesses your people.

2: He gives an order, and it comes quickly to the earth.

He sends snow as thick as wool,
and scatters frost like dust.
He sends hail like gravel;
no one can endure the cold he sends!
Then he gives a command, and melts the ice,
he sends the wind, and the water flows.

L: He gives his message to Jacob,
his instructions and laws to Israel.

U: *Praise the Lord!*

148

L: Praise the Lord!

2:    *Praise the Lord from heaven,*
   you that live in the heights above!
Praise him, all his angels, all his heavenly armies!

1:    *Praise him, sun and moon; praise him, shining stars!*
Praise him, highest heavens, and the waters above the sky!

2:    *Let them all praise the name of the Lord!*

He commanded, and they were created;
   by his command they were fixed in their places forever,
   and they cannot disobey.

1: Praise the Lord from the earth,
sea monsters and all ocean depths;
   lightning and hail, snow and clouds,
   strong winds that obey his command!

2: Praise him, hills and mountains, fruit trees and forests;
all animals, tame and wild; reptiles and birds!

1:    *Praise him, kings and all peoples,*
   princes and all other rulers;
   young men and girls,
   old people and children also!

2: Let them all praise the name of the Lord.
   His name is greater than all others;
   his glory is above earth and heaven!
He made his nation strong,

so that all his people praise him,
the people of Israel, so dear to him!

U: *Praise the Lord!*

149

L: Praise the Lord!

1: Sing a new song to the Lord;
   praise him in the meeting of his faithful people!

2: Be glad, Israel, because of your creator;
   rejoice, people of Zion, because of your king!

1: Praise his name with dancing;
   play drums and harps in praise of him.

2: The Lord takes pleasure in his people;
   he honors the humble with victory.
   *Let God's people rejoice in their triumph,
   and sing joyfully at their feasts.*

1: Let them shout aloud as they praise God.
   This is the victory of God's people!

U: *Praise the Lord!*

150

L: Praise the Lord!

1: Praise God in his temple!
   Praise his strength in heaven!
   Praise him for the mighty things he has done!
   Praise his supreme greatness!

2: Praise him with trumpets!
   Praise him with harps and lyres!
   Praise him with drums and dancing!
   Praise him with harps and flutes!
   Praise him with loud cymbals!

L: Praise the Lord, all living creatures!

U: *Praise the Lord!*

CALLS TO CONFESSION

1

L: Happy is the man who refuses the advice of evil men,
who does not follow the example of sinners,
or join those who make fun of God.

1: *Instead, he enjoys reading the law of the Lord,*
and studying it day and night.
He is like a tree that grows beside a stream;
it gives fruit at the right time,
and its leaves do not dry up.
He succeeds in everything he does.

2: *But evil men are not like this at all;*
they are like straw that the wind blows away.
Evil men will be condemned by God;
sinners will be kept apart from the righteous.

L: *The Lord cares for the righteous man,*
but the evil man will be lost forever.

2

L: Why do the nations plan rebellion?
Why do these people make useless plots?
Their kings revolt, their rulers plot together
against the Lord and his chosen king.

1: "Let us free ourselves from their rule," they say;
"let us throw off their control."

2: *From his throne in heaven the Lord laughs*
and makes fun of them.
He speaks to them in anger,
and terrifies them with his fury.
"On Zion, my sacred hill," he says,
"I have installed my king."

L: "I will announce what the Lord declared," says the king.
 "The Lord said to me: 'You are my son;
 today I have become your father.
 Ask, and I will give you all the nations;
 the whole earth will be yours.'"

1: Now listen to me, you kings;
 pay attention, you rulers!
 Serve the Lord with fear;
 tremble and bow down to him;

U: Happy are all who go to him for protection!

4

L: Answer me when I call, God my defender!

U: *When I was in trouble, you came to my help.*
 Be kind to me now and hear my prayer!

1: *How long will you men insult me?*
 How long will you love what is worthless,
 and go after what is false?
 Remember that the Lord has chosen me to be his own,
 and hears me when I call to him.

2: Be afraid and stop your sinning;
 think deeply about this, alone and silent in your rooms.
 Offer the right sacrifices to the Lord,
 and put your trust in him.

1: There are many who say, "How we wish to receive a blessing!
 Look on us with kindness, Lord!
 The joy that you give me is much greater
 than the joy of those who have plenty of grain and wine.

2: *As soon as I lie down, I go quietly to sleep;*
 you alone, Lord, keep me perfectly safe.

7:1

L: Lord, my God, I have found safety with you;
 save me and rescue me from all who pursue me,
 or else like a lion they will carry me off
 where no one can save me;
 there they will tear me to pieces.

1: Lord, my God, if I have done any of these:
   if I have wronged someone,
   if I have betrayed my friend,
   or without cause done violence to my enemy,
     help me, because justice is what you demand.
   Bring together all the peoples around you,
   and rule over them from above.
     You, Lord, are the judge of all men.

2: Stop the wickedness of evil men,
   and reward, I pray, the good men.
     You are a righteous God,
     and judge men's thoughts and desires.

   God is my protector; he saves those who obey him.
     God is a righteous judge
     and always condemns the wicked.

1: If men do not repent,
     God will sharpen his sword.
   He bends his bow and makes it ready;
     he takes up his deadly weapons
     and aims his burning arrows.

2: See how the wicked man thinks up evil;
   he plans trouble and practices deception.
     He digs a deep hole in the ground,
     then falls into his own pit!
   So he is punished by his own evil;
     he is hurt by his own violence.

10:1

L: Why are you so far away, Lord?
     Why do you hide yourself in times of trouble?
   The wicked are proud and persecute the poor;
     may they be caught in the traps they have made.

1: The wicked man brags about his evil desires;
     the greedy man curses and rejects the Lord.
   In his pride the wicked man says,
   "God will not punish me! He doesn't care!"
     This is what the wicked man thinks.

2: He succeeds in all he does.
　　He cannot understand God's judgments;
　he sneers at his enemies.
　　He says to himself, "I will never fail;
　　I will never be in trouble."
　His speech is filled with curses, lies, and threats;
　　he is quick to speak hateful and evil words.

1: He hides himself in the villages;
　　he waits there and murders innocent people.
　He spies on his helpless victim;
　　he waits in his hiding place like a lion.
　He lies in wait for his victim;
　　he catches him in his trap and drags him away.

2: The helpless victim lies crushed;
　　brute strength has defeated him.
　The wicked man says to himself, "God doesn't care!
　　He has closed his eyes, and will never see me!"

11

L: I trust in the Lord for safety.

2:　*How foolish of you to say to me,*
　　"Fly away like a bird to the mountains;
　the wicked draw their bows and aim their arrows
　to shoot at good men in the darkness.
　　There is nothing a good man can do
　　when things fall apart."

1: The Lord is in his holy temple;
　　he has his throne in heaven.
　He watches all men and knows what they do.
　　He examines both the good and the wicked;
　he hates the lawless with all his heart.

U:　*The Lord is righteous and loves good deeds;*
　　those who obey him will live in his presence.

14

L: Fools say to themselves, "God doesn't matter!"

1: *They are all corrupt,*
they have done terrible things;
        there is no one who does what is right.

2: The Lord looks down at men from heaven
to see if there are any who are wise,
any who worship him.
        But they have all gone wrong, they are all equally bad;
        not one of them does what is right, not a single one.

1: "Don't they know?" asks the Lord.
"Are all these evildoers ignorant?
        They live by robbing my people and do not pray to me."

2: But they will become terrified,
because God is with those who obey him.
        They make fun of the plans of the helpless man,
        because he trusts in the Lord.

U: How I pray that salvation will come to Israel from Zion!

15

L: Lord, who may live in your temple?
        Who may stay on Zion, your sacred hill?

1: The man who obeys God in everything,
and always does what is right;
whose words are true and sincere,
and who does not slander others.
        He does no wrong to his friends
        and does not spread rumors about his neighbors.

2: He despises those whom God rejects,
but honors those who obey the Lord.
        He always does what he promises,
        no matter how much it may cost him.
He cannot be bribed to testify against the innocent.

U: *He who does these things will never fail.*

18:20

L: The Lord rewards me because I am righteous;
        he blesses me because I am innocent.

1: I have obeyed the law of the Lord;
   I have not rebelled against my God.
   I have observed all his laws;
   I have not disobeyed his commands.
   He knows that I have kept myself from evil.
   He rewards me because I am righteous,
   because he knows that I am innocent.

2: You, Lord, are faithful to those who are faithful,
   and completely good to those who are perfect.
   You are pure to those who are pure,
   but hostile to those who are wicked.
   You save those who are humble;
   you humble those who are proud.

1: The Lord gives me light;
   my God dispels my darkness.
   He gives me strength to attack my enemies,
   the power to overcome their defenses.

U: *This God — how perfect are his deeds,*
    how dependable are his words!
   He is like a shield for all who seek his protection.

19:7

L: The law of the Lord is perfect; it gives new life.

1: *The commands of the Lord are trustworthy,*
    giving wisdom to those who lack it.
    The rules of the Lord are right,
    and those who obey them are happy.
    His commandments are completely just
    and give understanding to the mind.

2: The worship of the Lord is good;
   it will continue forever.
   The judgments of the Lord are just,
   they are always fair.
   They are more desirable than gold,
   even the finest gold.

They are sweeter than honey,
even the purest honey.
They give knowledge to me, your servant;
I am rewarded for obeying them.

1: *No one can see his own errors;*
deliver me from hidden faults!

2: Keep me safe, also, from open sins;
don't let them rule over me.
Then I shall be free from terrible sin.

U: *May my words and my thoughts be acceptable to you,*
O Lord, my refuge and my redeemer!

26

L: Declare that I am innocent, Lord,
because I do what is right and trust you completely.

2: *Examine me and test me, Lord;*
judge my desires and thoughts.
Your constant love guides me;
your faithfulness always leads me.

1: *I do not keep company with worthless men;*
I have nothing to do with hypocrites.
I hate the company of evil men and avoid the wicked.

2: Lord, I wash my hands to show that I am innocent
and march in worship around your altar.
I sing a hymn of thanksgiving
and tell all your wonderful deeds.

1: Lord, I love the house where you live,
the place where your glory dwells.
Do not destroy me with the sinners;
spare me from the fate of murderers —
men who do evil at all times
and are always ready to bribe.

U: As for me, I do what is right;
be merciful to me and save me!

27:7

L: Hear me, Lord, when I call to you!
Be merciful and answer me!

2: "Come to me," you said.
I will come to you, Lord;
don't hide yourself from me!

1: Don't be angry with me;
don't turn your servant away.
You have been my help;
don't leave me, don't abandon me, God, my Savior!

2: My father and mother may abandon me,
but the Lord will take care of me.

1: *Teach me, Lord, what you want me to do*
and lead me along a safe path,
because I have many enemies.
Do not abandon me to my enemies,
who attack me with lies and threats.

U: *Certainly I will live to see*
the Lord's goodness to his people.

L: Trust in the Lord! Have faith, don't despair.

U: *Trust in the Lord!*

33:8

L: Fear the Lord, all the earth!

U: *Fear him, all peoples of the world!*

1: When he spoke, the world was created;
at his command everything appeared.

2: The Lord frustrates the purposes of the nations;
he keeps them from carrying out their plans.

1: But his plans endure forever,
his purposes last eternally.

2: Happy is the nation whose God is the Lord;
happy are the people he has chosen for his own!

1: The Lord looks down from heaven and sees all mankind.

2:   *From where he rules he looks down*
     on all who live on earth,
     and knows everything they do.

36:1

L: Sin speaks to the wicked man deep in his heart;
     he rejects God, and does not fear him.

1: Because he has such a high opinion of himself,
   he thinks that God will not discover
   and condemn his sin.

2:   *His speech is evil and full of lies.*
     He makes evil plans as he lies in bed;
     his conduct is not good,
     and he does not reject what is evil.

1: Lord, your constant love reaches the heavens,
     your faithfulness extends to the skies.
     Your righteousness is firm like the great mountains.
     Your judgments are like the depths of the sea.
     You, Lord, care for men and animals.

2:   *How precious, God, is your constant love!*
     Men find protection under the shadow of your wings.
     They feast on the abundant food from your house;
     you give them to drink from the river of your goodness.

U: *You are the source of all life,*
     and because of your light we see the light.

37:1

L: Don't be worried on account of the wicked;
     don't be jealous of those who do wrong;
     they will disappear like grass that dries up;
     they will die like plants that wither.

2: Trust in the Lord and do good;
   live in the land and be safe.
     Seek your happiness with the Lord,
     and he will give you what you most desire.

1: Give yourself to the Lord;

trust in him, and he will help you;
he will cause your goodness to shine as the light
and your righteousness as the noonday sun.

2: Be calm before the Lord; wait patiently for him to act;
don't be worried about those who prosper
or those who succeed in their evil plans.

1: Don't be angry; don't get mad!
Don't be worried! It won't do you any good.

2: The wicked draw their swords and bend their bows
to kill the poor and needy,
to slaughter men who are good;
but they will be stabbed by their own swords,
and their bows will be smashed.

1: The little that a good man owns
is worth more than the wealth of all the wicked;
because the Lord will take away
the strength of the wicked.
but protect those who are good.

37:23

L: The Lord guides a man safely in the way he should go
and is pleased with his conduct.

U: *If he falls, he will not stay down,*
because the Lord will help him up.

L: Turn away from evil and do good,
and you will live in the land forever;

U: *the Lord loves what is right,*
and he does not abandon his faithful people.

L: The Lord saves righteous men
and protects them in times of trouble.

U: *He helps them and rescues them;*
he saves them from the wicked,
because they go to him for protection.

41:1

L: Happy is the man who is concerned for the poor;
the Lord will help him when he is in trouble.

1: The Lord will protect him and preserve his life;
he will make him happy in the land;
he will not abandon him to the power of his enemies.

2: *The Lord will help him when he is sick*
and restore him to health.

U: I said, "I have sinned against you, Lord;
be merciful to me and cure me!"

49:1

L: Hear this, everyone!
Listen, all people everywhere,
great and small alike,
rich and poor together.

2: A man can never redeem himself;
he cannot pay God the price for his life,
because the payment for a man's life is too great.
What he can pay will never be enough
to keep him from the grave,
to let him live forever.
He sees that even wise men die,
as well as foolish and stupid men.

1: See what happens to those who trust in themselves,
the fate of those who are satisfied with their wealth —
they are doomed to die like sheep,
and death will be their shepherd.

U: But God will save me;
he will take me from the power of death.

50

L: The Almighty God, the Lord, speaks;
he calls to the whole earth, from east to west.

U: God shines from Zion, the city perfect in its beauty.

1: *Our God is coming, but not in silence;*
a raging fire is in front of him,
a furious storm around him.
He calls heaven and earth as witnesses
to see him judge his people.

He says, "Gather my faithful people to me,
those who made a covenant with me
by offering a sacrifice."
The heavens proclaim that God is righteous,
that he himself is judge!

2: "Listen, my people, and I will speak;
I will testify against you, Israel.
I am God, your God.
I do not reprimand you because of your sacrifices
and the burnt offerings you always bring me.
And yet, I do not need bulls from your farms,
or goats from your flocks,
because the animals of the woods are mine
and the cattle on thousands of hills.
All the wild birds are mine
and all living things in the fields.

1: *"If I were hungry I would not tell you,*
because the world and everything in it is mine.
Do I eat the flesh of bulls,
or drink the blood of goats?
Let the giving of thanks be your sacrifice to God,
and give the Almighty
all the offerings that you promised.
Call to me when trouble comes;
I will save you, and you will praise me."

2: But God says to the wicked,
"Why should you recite my commandments?
Why should you talk about my covenant?
You refuse to let me correct you;
you reject my commands.
When you see a thief, you become his friend,
and you associate with adulterers.

1: *"You are always ready to speak evil;*
you never hesitate to tell lies.
You are ready to accuse your own brothers,
and to find fault with them.
You have done all this, and I have said nothing,

so you thought that I am like you.
But now I will reprimand you,
and make the matter plain to you.

L: "Listen to this, you that ignore me,
or I will destroy you;
and there will be no one to save you.

U: *"Giving thanks is the sacrifice that honors me,*
and I will surely save all who obey me."

52

L: Why do you boast, great man, of your evil?
God's love is constant.

1: You make plans to ruin others;
your tongue is like a sharp razor.
You are always inventing lies.
You love evil more than good
and falsehood more than the truth.
You love to hurt people with your words, you liar!

2: So God will ruin you forever;
he will take hold of you and pull you out of your tent;
he will remove you from the land of the living.

1:   *Righteous people will see this and be afraid;*
they will say,
"Look, here is a man
who did not depend on God for safety,
but instead trusted in his great wealth,
and looked for security in being wicked!"

2: But I am like an olive tree growing
near the house of God;
I trust in his constant love forever and ever.
I will always thank you, God, for what you have done;

U: *in the company of your people*
I will proclaim that you are good.

58:1

L: Do you really give a just decision, you rulers?
Do you judge all men fairly?

1: No! You think only of the evil you will do,
and commit crimes of violence in the land.

2: *Evil men go wrong all their lives;*
they tell lies from the day they are born.

1: *They are full of poison, like snakes;*
they stop up their ears, life a deaf cobra.

2: *Break their teeth, God;*
tear out the fangs of these fierce lions, Lord!

U: *There is indeed a God who judges the world!*

62

L: I depend on God alone;
my salvation comes from him.

U: He alone is my protector and Savior;
he is my defender, and I shall never be defeated.

1: How much longer will all of you
attack a man to defeat him,
like a falling wall,
like a broken-down fence?

2: *You only want to bring him down*
from his place of honor;
you take pleasure in lies.
You speak words of blessing,
but in your heart you curse him.

1: I depend on God alone;
I put my hope in him.
He alone is my protector and Savior;
he is my defender, and I shall never be defeated.

2: My salvation and honor depend on God;
he is my strong protector; he is my shelter.

L: My people, trust in God at all times!

U: *Tell him all your troubles, because he is our refuge.*

1: Men are like a puff of breath;
mortal men are worthless.
Put them on the scales and they weigh nothing;
they are lighter than a mere breath.

2: Don't put your trust in violence;
   don't hope to gain anything by robbery;
   even if your riches increase,
   don't depend on them.

L: More than once I have heard God say
   that power belongs to him,
   and that his love is constant.

U: *You yourself, Lord, reward every man*
   according to his deeds.

65:1

L: God, people must praise you in Zion
   and give you what they have promised;

U: *you answer prayers.*

L: All men shall come to you on account of their sins.

U: *Our faults defeat us, but you forgive them.*

75

L: We praise you, God, we praise you!

1: *We proclaim how great you are,*
   and tell the wonderful things you have done!

2: "I have set a time for judgment," says God,
   "and I will judge with fairness.
   Though the earth and all who live on it disappear,
   I will keep its foundations firm.

1: "I tell the proud not to brag,
   and the wicked not to be arrogant;
   I tell them to quit showing off,
   and to stop their bragging."

2: Judgment does not come from the east or from the west,
   from the north or from the south;
   it is God who does the judging,
   putting some down and lifting others up.

1: The Lord holds a cup in his hand,
   full of fresh wine, very strong;
   he pours it out, and all the wicked drink it;
   they drink it down to the last drop.

2: I will never stop speaking of the God of Jacob,
   or singing praises to him.
   He will break the power of the wicked,
   but the power of the righteous will be increased.

80:1

L: Listen to us, Shepherd of Israel;

U: *hear us, leader of your flock.*

1: Seated on your throne, reveal your love.
   Show us your strength; come and save us!

2: Turn to us, Almighty God!
   Look down from heaven at us;
   come and save your grapevine!

U: Bring us back, Lord God Almighty!
   Show us your love, and we will be saved!

82

L: God presides in the heavenly council;
   in the meeting of the gods he gives his decision:

1: *"You must stop judging unjustly,*
   and quit being partial to the wicked!
   Defend the rights of the poor and the orphans;
   be fair to the needy and the helpless.
   Rescue the poor and the needy;
   save them from the power of evil men!

2: "How ignorant you are, how stupid!
   You live in darkness,
   and justice has disappeared from the world.
   I told you that you are gods,
   that all of you are the sons of the Most High.
   But you will die like men;
   your life will end like any prince."

U: Come, God, and rule the world;
   all the nations are yours.

94:3

L: How much longer will the wicked be glad?
   How much longer, Lord?

2: How much longer will evildoers be proud
and boast about their crimes?

1: *They crush your people, Lord;*
they oppress those who belong to you.
They kill widows and orphans,
and murder the strangers who live in our land.

2: *They say, "The Lord doesn't see us;*
the God of Israel does not notice!"

1: My people, how can you be such stupid fools?
When will you ever learn?
God made our ears—can't he hear?
He made our eyes—can't he see?

2: He is in charge of the nations—won't he punish them?
He is the teacher of all men—doesn't he know?
The Lord knows what they think;
he knows how senseless their reasoning is.

112

L: Praise the Lord!

1: *Happy is the man who fears the Lord,*
who takes pleasure in obeying his commands.
Light shines in the darkness for good men,
for those who are kind, merciful, and just.

2: *Happy is the man who is generous in his loans,*
who runs his business honestly.
A good man will never fail;
he will never be forgotten.

1: He is not afraid of receiving bad news;
his faith is strong, and he trusts in the Lord.
He is not worried or afraid;
he is certain he will see his enemies defeated.

2: He gives generously to the needy,
and his kindness is eternal.

119:1

L: Happy are those whose lives are faultless,
who live according to the law of the Lord.

1: *Happy are those who follow his commands,*
    who obey him with all their heart.
    Surely they do no wrong;
        they walk in the Lord's ways.

2: You have given us your laws,
    and told us to obey them faithfully.
        How I hope that I shall be faithful
        in keeping your rules!
    If I pay attention to all your commandments,
    then I will not be disappointed.
        As I learn your righteous rulings,
        I will praise you with a pure heart.

U: I will obey your laws;
        don't ever abandon me!

119:9

L: How can a young man keep his life pure?

U: *By obeying your commands, Lord.*

1: With all my heart I try to serve you;
        keep me from disobeying your commandments!
    I keep your law in my heart,
    so that I will not sin against you.
        I praise you, Lord: teach me your rules!

2: I will repeat aloud all the laws you have given.
        I delight in following your commands,
        more than in having great wealth.
    I study your instructions; I examine your teachings.

U: *I take pleasure in your laws,*
    I will not forget your commands.

119:17

L: Be good to me, your servant,
    so that I may live and obey your teachings.

1: *Open my eyes, so that I may see*
    the wonderful truths in your law.
    I am here on earth for just a little while;
        do not hide your commandments from me!

My heart aches with longing;
at all times I want to know your judgments.

2: You reprimand the proud;
cursed are those who depart from your commands.

1: Free me from their insults and scorn,
because I have kept your laws.
Even though the rulers meet and plot against me,
I, your servant, will study your rules.

2: Your instructions give me pleasure;
they are my advisers.
With all my heart I try to serve you;
keep me from disobeying your commandments.

119:33

L: Teach me, Lord, the meaning of your laws,
and I will obey them at all times.
Explain your law to me, and I will obey it;
I will keep it with all my heart.

1: Lead me in the way of your commandments,
because in them I find happiness.
Make me want to obey your rules,
rather than to get rich.

2: Keep me from paying attention to what is worthless;
be good to me, as you have promised.

1: Keep your promise to me, your servant,
which you make to those who fear you.
Save me from the insults which I fear;
how wonderful your rules are!

2: I want to obey your commands;
because you are righteous, be good to me!

119:114

L: You are my defender and protector;
I hope in your promise.

1: Give me strength, as you promised, and I shall live;
don't let me be disappointed in my hope!

2: Hold me, and I will be safe,
I will always pay attention to your commands.

1: Because of you, I am afraid;

2: *I am filled with fear because of your judgments.*

119:161

L: Powerful men attack me unjustly,
but it is your law that I respect.

1: *How happy I am because of your promises,*
as happy as someone who finds rich treasure.

2: I hate and detest all lies, but I love your law.
Seven times each day I thank you
for your righteous judgments.

1: Those who love your law have complete security,
and there is nothing that can make them fall.

2: *I wait for you to save me, Lord,*
and I do what you command.
I obey your rules;
I love them with all my heart.

U: I obey your commands and your instructions;
you see everything I do.

120

L: When I was in trouble I called to the Lord,
and he answered me.

1: *Save me, Lord, from liars and deceivers!*

2: You liars, what will God do to you?
How will he punish you?
With a soldier's sharp arrows,
with red-hot charcoals!
I have lived too long with people who hate peace!

1: *When I speak of peace, they are for war.*

U: When I was in trouble I called to the Lord
and he answered me.
Save me, Lord!

123:1

L: Lord, I look up to you,
  up to heaven, where you rule.

U: *As the servant depends on his master,*
  and the maid depends on her mistress,
  so we keep looking to you, Lord our God,
  until you have mercy on us.

L: Be merciful to us, Lord, be merciful.

139

L: Lord, you have examined me, and you know me.

1: *You know everything I do;*
  from far away you understand all my thoughts.
  You see me, whether I am working or resting;
  you know all my actions.

2: *Even before I speak*
  you already know what I will say.
  You are all around me, on every side;
  you protect me with your power.
  Your knowledge of me is overwhelming;
  it is too deep for me to understand.

1: Where could I go to escape from your Spirit?
  Where could I get away from your presence?

2: If I went up to heaven, you would be there;
  if I lay down in the world of the dead,
  you would be there.
  If I flew away beyond the east,
  or lived in the farthest place in the west,
  you would be there to lead me,
  you would be there to help me.

1: I could ask the darkness to hide me,
  or the light around me to turn into night,
  but even the darkness is not dark for you,
  and the night is as bright as the day.
  Darkness and light are the same to you.

2: You created every part of me;
   you put me together in my mother's womb.
   I praise you because you are to be feared;
   all you do is strange and wonderful.
   I know it with all my heart.
   You saw my bones being formed,
   carefully put together in my mother's womb,
   when I was growing there in secret.
   You saw me before I was born.
   The days that had been created for me
   had all been recorded in your book,
   before any of them had ever begun.

1: *God, how difficult your thoughts are for me;*
   how many of them there are!
   If I counted them, they would be more
   than the grains of sand.
   When I awake, I am still with you.

2: Examine me, God, and know my mind;
   test me, and discover my thoughts.
   Find out if there is any deceit in me,
   and guide me in the eternal way.

PSALMS OF CONFESSION

19:12

1: No one can see his own errors;
   deliver me from hidden faults!

2: Keep me safe, also, from open sins;
   don't let them rule over me.
   Then I shall be perfect
   and free from terrible sin.

U: *May my words and my thoughts be acceptable to you,*
   O Lord, my refuge and my redeemer!

25:1

L: To you, Lord, I offer my prayer;
   in you, my God, I trust.

2: Teach me your ways, Lord,
   make them known to me.
   Teach me to live according to your truth,
   because you are my Savior.
   All day long I trust in you.

1: Lord, remember your kindness and constant love,
   which you have shown from long ago.
   Forgive the sins and errors of my youth.
   Because of your constant love and goodness,
   remember me, Lord!

2: Keep your promise, Lord,
   and forgive my sins, because they are many.
   Turn to me, Lord, and be merciful to me,
   because I am alone and weak.
   Relieve me of all my worries
   and save me from all my troubles.

1: Consider all my distress and suffering
  and forgive all my sins.
  Protect me and save me;
    keep me from defeat,
    because I come to you for protection.

U: *From all their troubles, save your people, God!*

28:1

L: Lord, my defender, I call to you. Hear my cry!

1: *If you do not answer me,*
    I will be among those who go down
    to the land of the dead.

2: Hear me when I cry to you for help,
  with my hands lifted toward your holy temple.

1: *Do not condemn me with the wicked,*
    with those who do evil.

2: Save your people, Lord, and bless those who are yours!
    Be their shepherd, and take care of them forever.

38:1

L: Lord, don't be angry and rebuke me!

2: *Don't punish me in your anger!*
  I am drowning in the flood of my sins;
    I am weighted down by their heavy burden.

1: Because I have been foolish,
  I am bent over, I am crushed; I mourn all day long.

2: *I am utterly crushed and defeated;*
    my heart is troubled, and I groan with pain.

1: Lord, you know what I desire; you hear all my groans.
    My heart is pounding, my strength is gone,
    and my eyes have lost their brightness.

2: My friends and neighbors will not come near me;
    even my family stays away from me.

1: I am like a deaf man, and cannot hear,
  like a dumb man, and cannot speak;
    I am like a man who does not answer,
    because he cannot hear.

2: I trust in you, Lord;
and you, Lord my God, will answer me.
I am about to fall,
and my pain is always with me.

I confess my sins,
and they fill me with anxiety.

1: Do not abandon me, Lord;

2: do not stay away, my God!

U: *Help me now, Lord my Savior!*

40:12

L: I am surrounded by many troubles—too many to count!

U: *My sins have caught up with me,*
and I can no longer see;
they are more than the hairs on my head,
and I have lost my courage.

1: *Save me, Lord! Help me now!*

2: I am weak and helpless, but you, Lord, think of me.

U: *You are my helper and Savior—do not delay, my God!*

41:4

L: I have sinned against you, Lord;
U: *be merciful to me and cure me!*

1: Be merciful to me, Lord,

2: *and restore my health.*

U: You will help me;
you will keep me in your presence forever.

51:1

L: Be merciful to me, God,
because of your constant love;
wipe away my sins,
because of your great mercy!

1: Wash away my evil,
and make me clean from my sin!

2: I recognize my faults;
I am always conscious of my sins.

1: *I have sinned against you—only against you,*
    and done what you consider evil.
    So you are right in judging me;
    you are justified in condemning me.

2: I have been evil from the time I was born;
    from the day of my birth I have been sinful.

1: A faithful heart is what you want;
    fill my mind with your wisdom.

2: Remove my sin, and I will be clean;
    wash me, and I will be whiter than snow.

L: Let me hear the sounds of joy and gladness;
    and though you have crushed and broken me,
    I will be happy once again.

U: *Close your eyes to my sins,*
    and wipe out all my evil.

51:10

L: Create a pure heart in me, God,
    and put a new and loyal spirit in me.

1: Do not banish me from your presence;
    do not take your Holy Spirit away from me.
    Give me again the joy that comes from your salvation,
    and make my spirit obedient.

2: *Help me to speak, Lord, and I will praise you.*
    You do not want sacrifices,
    or I would offer them;
    you are not pleased with burnt offerings.

U: *My sacrifice is a submissive spirit, God;*
    a submissive and obedient heart you will not reject.

69:5

1: My sins, God, are not hidden from you;
    you know how foolish I have been!
    Don't let me bring shame to those who trust in you,
    Lord God Almighty!
    Don't let me bring disgrace to those who worship you,
    God of Israel!

2: But as for me, I will pray to you, Lord;
   answer me, God, at a time you choose,
   because of your great love,
   because you keep your promise to save.
   Save me from sinking in the mud.

U: *Answer me, Lord, in the goodness of your constant love;*
    in your great compassion, turn to me!

70

L: Save me, God!
   Lord, help me now!

1: May all who come to you be glad and joyful!

2: *May all who love your salvation*
   always say, "How great God is!"

1: I am weak and helpless;
   come quickly to me, God.

2: You are my helper and Savior—
   do not delay, Lord!

79:8

1: Do not punish us for the sins of our ancestors,
   but have mercy on us now,
   because we have lost all hope.

2: Listen to the groans of the prisoners,
   and by your great power
   free those who are condemned to die.

U: *And we, your people, the sheep of your flock,*
    will thank you forever
    and praise you for all time to come.

106:4

L: Remember me, Lord, when you help your people;
   include me, when you save them.

2: We have sinned, as our ancestors did;
   we have been wicked and evil.
   Our ancestors in Egypt did not understand
   God's wonderful acts;

they forgot the many times
he showed his love for them,
and they rebelled against the Almighty
at the Sea of Reeds.

1: They quickly forgot what he had done,
and acted without waiting for his advice.
They defiled themselves by their actions,
and were unfaithful to God.

2: Many times the Lord rescued his people,
but they chose to rebel against him,
and sank deeper into sin.

1: *Yet the Lord heard them when they cried out,*
and took notice of their distress.
For their sake he remembered his covenant,
and because of his great love he changed his mind.

U: *Save us, Lord our God,*
and bring us back from among the nations,
so that we may praise your holy name,
and be happy in thanking you.

119:25

1: I lie defeated in the dust;
revive me, as you have promised!
I confessed all I have done, and you answered me;
teach me your rules!

2: Teach me how to obey your laws,
and I will study your wonderful teachings.
I am overcome by sorrow;
strengthen me, as you have promised.

1: Keep me from going the wrong way,
and in your goodness teach me your law.
I have decided to be obedient.

2: *I will eagerly obey your commands,*
because you will give me more understanding.

119:124

L: Treat me according to your constant love,
and teach me your commands.

*I am your servant, so give me understanding
that I may know your teachings.*

1: Lord, it is time for you to act,
because people are disobeying your law!
*My tears pour down like a river,
because people do not obey your law.*

2: Turn to me and have mercy on me
as you do on those who love you.
*Keep me from falling, as you have promised;
don't let me be overcome by evil.*

U: *Bless me with your presence, and teach me your laws.*

119:169

L: Let my cry for help reach you, Lord!
Give me understanding, as you have promised.

U: Let my prayer come before you,
and save me, according to your promise!

1: How I long for your salvation, Lord!

2: *Give me life, so that I may praise you.*

U: *I wander about like a lost sheep;
so come and look for me, your servant.*

130

L: In my despair I call to you, Lord.

1: *Hear my cry, Lord, listen to my call for help!*
If you kept a record of our sins,
who could escape being condemned?
But you forgive us, so that we should fear you.

2: I wait eagerly for the Lord's help,
and in his word I trust.
*I wait for the Lord,
more eagerly than watchmen wait for the dawn.*

L: Israel, trust in the Lord; his love is constant,
and he is always willing to save.

U: *He will save his people Israel
from all their sins.*

PSALMS OF ASSURANCE

18:4

1: Death pulled its ropes tight around me;
   the waves of destruction rolled over me.
   Death pulled its ropes tight around me,
   and the grave set its trap for me.

2: In my trouble I called to the Lord;
   I called to my God for help.
   In his temple he heard my voice;
   my cry for help reached his ears.

U: The Lord gives me light;
   my God dispels my darkness.

28:6

L: Give praise to the Lord;
   he has heard my cry for help!

1: The Lord protects and defends me;
   I trust in him.
   He helped me, and so I am glad
   and sing hymns of praise to him.

2: The Lord protects his people;
   he defends and saves his chosen king.

U: Save your people, Lord,
   and bless those who are yours!
   Be their shepherd,
   and take care of them forever.

31:21

L: Praise the Lord!

U: *How wonderfully he showed his love for me.*

L: I was afraid, and thought
that you had thrown me out of your presence.

U: *But you heard my cry,*
      when I called to you for help.

L: Love the Lord, all his faithful people!

U: *Be strong, be courageous,*
      all who hope in the Lord!

32

L: Happy is the man whose sins are forgiven,
whose transgressions are pardoned.

2:    *Happy is the man*
      whom the Lord does not accuse of doing wrong,
      who is free from all deceit.

1: When I did not confess my sins,
I was worn out from crying all day long.
      Day and night you punished me, Lord;
      my strength was completely drained,
      as moisture is dried up by the summer heat.

2: Then I confessed my sins to you;
      I did not conceal my wrongdoings.
I decided to confess them to you,
      and you forgave all my transgressions.

1: So all your loyal people should pray to you
in times of need;
      when a great flood comes rushing,
      it will not reach them.

2: You are my hiding place;
you will save me from trouble.
      I sing aloud of your salvation,
      because you protect me.

1: The Lord says, "I will teach you the way you should go;
I will instruct you and advise you.
      Don't be stupid like a horse or a mule,

which must be controlled with a bit and bridle,
to make it obey you."

2: The wicked will have to suffer,
   but those who trust in the Lord
   are protected by his constant love.
   All who are righteous, be glad and rejoice,
   because of what the Lord has done!

U: *All who obey him, shout for joy!*

55:16

L: I call to the Lord God for help,
   and he will save me.

1:    *My complaints and groans*
      go up to him morning, noon, and night,
      and he will hear my voice.

2: Leave your troubles with the Lord,
   and he will support you.

U: *As for me, I will trust in God.*

62:1

L: I depend on God alone;
   my salvation comes from him.

U: He alone is my protector and Savior;
   he is my defender,
   and I shall never be defeated.

65:1

L: God, people must praise you in Zion
   and give you what they have promised
   because you answer prayers.
   All men shall come to you on account of their sins.

1:    *Our faults defeat us, but you forgive them.*

2: Happy are those whom you choose,
   whom you bring to live in your sanctuary!

U: *We shall be satisfied*
   with the good things of your house,
   the blessings of your sacred temple!

66:16

L: Come and listen, all who honor God,
   and I will tell you what he has done for me.

1: *I cried to him for help;*
   I was ready to praise him with songs.
   If I had ignored my sins,
   the Lord would not have listened to me.

2: *But God has indeed heard me;*
   he has listened to my prayer.

U: I praise God, because he did not reject my prayer,
   or keep back his constant love from me.

85:1

L: Lord, you have been kind to your land;

1: *You have forgiven your people's sins*
   and pardoned all their wrongs.

2: I am listening to what the Lord God is saying;
   he promises peace to us, his own people,
   if we do not go back to our foolish ways.

U: Please renew our strength,
   and we, your people, will praise you.
   Show us your constant love, Lord,
   and give us your saving help.

91:14

L: God says, "I will save those who love me,
   and protect those who know me.

U: *"When they call to me, I will answer them;*
   when they are in trouble, I will be with them.
   I will rescue them and honor them.
   I will surely save them."

94:17

L: If the Lord had not helped me,
   I would have gone quickly to the land of silence.

U: *I said, "I am falling";*

but, Lord, your constant love held me up.
When I am anxious and worried,
you comfort me and make me glad.

99:8

L: Lord, our God, you answered your people;
  you showed them that you are a God who forgives.

U: Praise the Lord our God
  and worship at his sacred mountain!
  The Lord our God is holy!

103:8

L: The Lord is merciful and loving,
  slow to become angry, and full of constant love.
  He does not keep on reprimanding;
  he is not angry forever.

U: *He does not punish us as we deserve,*
  or repay us for our sins and wrongs.
  As high as the sky is above the earth,
  so great is his love for those who fear him.
  As far as the east is from the west,
  so far does he remove our sins from us.

107:10

1: Some were living in gloom and darkness,
  prisoners suffering in chains;
    they had rebelled against the commands
    of Almighty God,
    and had rejected his instructions.
  They were worn out from hard work;
  they would fall down and no one would help.

2: *In their trouble they called to the Lord,*
  and he saved them from their distress.
  He brought them out of their gloom and darkness,
  and smashed their chains.

1: *They must thank the Lord for his constant love,*
  for the wonderful things he did for them.
  He breaks down bronze doors, and smashes iron bars.

2:    *Some were sick because of their sins,*
     suffering because of their evil;
     they couldn't stand the sight of food,
     and were close to dying.

1:    *In their trouble they called to the Lord,*
     and he saved them from their distress.
     He healed them with his command,
     and saved them from the grave.

2:    *They must thank the Lord for his constant love,*
     for the wonderful things he did for them.

U: They must thank him with sacrifices,
     and with songs of joy tell all he has done!

119:114

L: Give me strength, as you promised, and I shall live;
     you are my defender and protector.
     I hope in your promise.

U: *Hold me, and I will be safe,*
     and I will always pay attention to your commands.

119:153

L: Look at my suffering, and save me;
     I have not neglected your law.

1: Defend my cause, and set me free;
     save me, as you have promised!

2: The wicked will not be saved;
     they do not obey your laws;
     but your compassion, Lord, is great,
     so save me, according to your decision.

U: I love your instructions, Lord!
     save me, according to your constant love.

130

L: In my despair I call to you, Lord.

1:    *Hear my cry, Lord,*
     listen to my call for help!

If you kept a record of our sins,
who could escape being condemned?
But you forgive us,
so that we should fear you.

2: I wait eagerly for the Lord's help,
and in his word I trust.
I wait for the Lord,
more eagerly than watchmen wait for the dawn.

L: Israel, trust in the Lord,
because his love is constant,
and he is always willing to save.

U: *He will save his people Israel*
from all their sins.

131

L: Lord, I have given up my pride,
and turned from my arrogance.

1: *I am not concerned with great matters,*
or with subjects too difficult for me.
But I am content and at peace.

2: As a child lies quietly in its mother's arms,
so my heart is quiet within me.

U: *Israel, trust in the Lord,*
from now on and forever!

PREPARATION FOR THE WORD

19:7

L: The law of the Lord is perfect; it gives new life.

1: *The commands of the Lord are trustworthy,*
giving wisdom to those who lack it.
The rules of the Lord are right,
and those who obey them are happy.
His commandments are completely just
and give understanding to the mind.

2: The worship of the Lord is good;
it will continue forever.
The judgments of the Lord are just,
they are always fair.
They are more desirable than gold,
even the finest gold.
They are sweeter than honey,
even the purest honey.
They give knowledge to me, your servant.

U: *May my words and my thoughts be acceptable to you,*
O Lord, my refuge and my redeemer!

119:33

L: Teach me, Lord, the meaning of your laws,
and I will obey them at all times.
Explain your law to me, and I will obey it;
I will keep it with all my heart.

1: Lead me in the way of your commandments,
because in them I find happiness.
Make me want to obey your rules,
rather than to get rich.

2: Keep me from paying attention to what is worthless;
   be good to me, as you have promised.
   I want to obey your commands.

U: *Keep your promise to me, your servant,*
    which you make to those who fear you.

119:41

L: Show me how much you love me, Lord,
   and save me according to your promise.
   I trust in your word.
   Enable me to speak the true message at all times,
   because my hope is in your judgments.

1: I will always obey your law, forever and ever!
   I will live in complete freedom,
   because I have tried to obey your rules.

2: I will announce your commands to kings,
   and I will not be ashamed.
   I find pleasure in obeying your commandments,
   because I love them.

U: I respect and love your commandments;
   I will meditate on your instructions.

119:49

L: Remember your promise to me, your servant;
   it has given me hope.

1: *Even in my suffering I was comforted,*
    because your promise gave me life.

2: I remember the instructions you gave me in the past,
   and they bring me comfort, Lord.

1: *Living far away from my real home,*
    I compose songs about your commands.

2: In the night I think of you, Lord, and I obey your law.
   This is my happiness: I obey your commands.

1: You are all I want, Lord; I promise to obey your laws.

2: *I ask you with all my heart:*
    Have mercy on me, as you have promised!

119:64

L: Lord, the earth is full of your constant love;
teach me your commandments!

1: You created me, and you keep me safe;
give me understanding, so that I may learn your laws.

2: Let your constant love comfort me,
as you have promised me, your servant.
Have mercy on me, and I will live,
because I take pleasure in your law.

119:97

L: How I love your law!
I think about it all day long.

1: Your commandment is with me all the time.
I want to obey your word.
I have not neglected your instructions,
because it was you who taught me.

2: *Your word is a lamp to guide me,*
and a light for my path.
I will keep my solemn promise
to obey your righteous instructions.

1: *Accept my prayer of thanks, Lord,*
and teach me your commands.
I am always ready to risk my life;
I have not forgotten your law.

2: Your commandments are my eternal possession;
they are the joy of my heart.

119:124

L: Treat me according to your constant love,
and teach me your commands.

1: *I am your servant, so give me understanding*
that I may know your teachings.

2: Your teachings are wonderful;
I obey them with all my heart.
The explanation of your teachings gives light,
and brings wisdom to the inexperienced.

U: *Bless me with your presence,*
    and teach me your laws.

119:137

L: You are righteous, Lord,
   and your laws are right.

2: *How certain your promise is!*
    How much your servant loves it!

1: Your righteousness will last forever,
   and your law is always true.

U: Your instructions are righteous forever;
   give me understanding, and I shall live.

PSALMS OF SUPPLICATION

6:1

L: Lord, don't be angry and rebuke me!
  Don't punish me in your anger!
  Have pity on me, because I am worn out;
  restore me, because I am completely exhausted;
  my whole being is deeply troubled.
  How long, Lord, will this last?

1: Come and save me, Lord;
  because you love me, rescue me from death.

2: I am worn out with grief;
  every night my bed is damp from my crying,
  my pillow is soaked with tears.

U: The Lord hears my weeping;
  he listens to my cries for help,
  and answers my prayers.

9:13

L: Be merciful to me, Lord!
  See how mistreated I am by those who hate me!

1: Rescue me from death, Lord,
  that I may stand before the people of Jerusalem
  and tell them all the things for which I praise you.
  I will rejoice because you saved me.

2: The heathen have dug a pit and fallen in;
  they have set a trap and been caught in it.
  The Lord has revealed himself by his righteous judgments,
  and the wicked are trapped by their own deeds.
  Death is the destiny of all the wicked,
  of all those who reject God.

1: *The needy will not always be neglected;*
the hope of the oppressed will not be crushed forever.
Come, Lord! Don't let men defy you!
Bring the heathen before you and judge them.

2: Make them afraid, Lord;
make them know that they are only men.

10:12

L: Come, Lord, and save me!
Don't forget the oppressed, God!

1: How can the wicked man despise God,
and say to himself, "He will not punish me"?

2: *But you do see; you take notice of suffering and grief*
and are always ready to help.
The helpless man commits himself to you,
because you have always helped the needy.

1: Break the power of wicked and evil men.
The Lord is king forever and ever,
and the heathen will disappear from his land.

2: You will listen, Lord, to the prayers of the lowly;
you will give them courage.
You will hear the cries of the oppressed and the orphans
and judge in their favor,
so that mortal men may cause terror no more.

12

L: Save me, Lord!

1: *There are no good men left,*
and honest men can no longer be found.
All men lie to one another,
and deceive each other with flattery.

2: *Silence those flattering tongues, Lord,*
and close those boastful mouths!
They say, "We will speak as we wish,
and no one will stop us.
Who can tell us what to say?"

1: *"But now I will come," says the Lord,*
"because the needy are oppressed,
and the persecuted groan in pain.
I will give them the security they long for!"

L: *The Lord's promises can be trusted;*
they are as genuine as silver,
refined seven times in the furnace.

U: *Keep us always safe, Lord,*
and preserve us from such people.

2: Wicked men are everywhere,
and everyone praises what is evil.

L: Save me, Lord!

U: *Keep us always safe!*

13

L: How long will you forget me, Lord? Forever?
How much longer will you hide yourself from me?

1: How long must I endure pain?
How long will sorrow fill my heart day and night?
How long will my enemies triumph over me?

2: *Look at me, Lord my God, and answer me.*
Restore my strength, so that I will not die.
Then my enemies cannot say, "We have defeated him!"
They cannot be glad over my downfall.

U: *But I rely on your constant love;*
I will be glad, because you will save me.
I will sing to the Lord,
because he has been good to me.

16

L: Protect me, God, because I come to you for safety.

2: *I say to the Lord, "You are my Lord;*
all the good things I have come from you."
How excellent are the Lord's faithful people!
My greatest pleasure is to be with them.

1: Those who rush to other gods
   bring troubles on themselves.
   I will not take part in their sacrifices;
   I will not worship their gods.

2: You, Lord, are all I have,
   and you give me all I need; my life is in your hands.
   How wonderful are your gifts to me; how good they are!

1: *I praise the Lord, because he guides me,*
   and in the night my conscience warns me.
   I am always aware of the Lord's presence;
   he is near, and nothing can shake me.

2: And so I am full of happiness and joy,
   and I always feel secure;
   because you will not allow me
   to go to the world of the dead,
   you will not abandon to the depths below
   the one you love.

U: *You will show me the path that leads to life;*
   your presence fills me with joy,
   and your help brings pleasure forever.

17

L: Listen, Lord, to my righteous plea;
   pay attention to my cry for help!

1: *Listen to my prayer, because there is no deceit in me.*
   You will judge in my favor,
   because you know what is right. .

2: *You know my heart; you come to me at night.*
   You have examined me completely;
   I speak no evil, as others do;
   I have obeyed your command
   and have not followed the path of violence.
   I have always walked in your way
   and have not strayed from it.

1: I pray to you, God, because you answer me;
   so turn to me and listen to my words.

Reveal your wonderful love, Savior;
  at your side we are safe from our enemies.
Protect me, as you would your very eyes;
  hide me in the shadow of your wings
  from the attacks of the wicked.

2: My enemies, full of hate, surround me;
  they have no pity and speak proudly.
  Now they are around me wherever I turn,
  watching for a chance to pull me down.
    They are like lions, wanting to tear me to pieces,
    like young lions, waiting for me in their hiding places.

1: Come, Lord, oppose my enemies and defeat them!
  Save me from them by your power.

U: Because I am righteous, I will see you;
  when I awake, your presence will fill me with joy.

22:1

L: My God, my God, why have you abandoned me?

1: *I have cried desperately for help,*
    but it still does not come!
  During the day I call to you, my God,
  but you do not answer;
    I call at night, but get no rest.

2: But you are enthroned as the Holy One,
    the one whom Israel praises.
    Our ancestors put their trust in you;
    they trusted you, and you saved them.
  They called to you and escaped from danger;
    they trusted in you and were not disappointed.

1: But I am no longer a man;
    I am a worm, despised and scorned by all!
  All who see me make fun of me;
    they stick out their tongues and shake their heads.
  "You relied on the Lord," they say,
  "Why doesn't he save you?
    If the Lord likes you, why doesn't he help you?"

2: It was you who brought me safely through birth,
   and when I was a baby you kept me safe.
   I have relied on you ever since I was born;
   since my birth you have been my God.
   Do not stay away from me!
   Trouble is near, and there is no one to help.

1: Many enemies surround me like bulls;
   they are all around me.
   They open their mouths like lions,
   roaring and tearing at me.
   My strength is gone,
   gone like water spilled on the ground.
   All my bones are out of joint;
   my heart feels like melted wax inside me.

2: My throat is as dry as dust,
   and my tongue sticks to the roof of my mouth.
   You have left me for dead in the dust.
   A gang of evil men is around me;
   like a pack of dogs, they close in on me;
   they tear my hands and feet.

1:   *All my bones can be seen.*
   My enemies look at me and stare;
   they divide my clothes among themselves
   and gamble for my robe.

U: Don't stay away from me, Lord!
   Hurry and help me, my Savior!

31:1

L: I come to you, Lord, for protection;
   never let me be defeated.

1:   *You are a righteous God; save me, I pray!*
   Hear me! Save me now!
   Be my refuge, to protect me; my defense, to save me.

2: You are my refuge and defense;
   guide me and lead me as you have promised.
   Keep me safe from the trap that has been set for me;
   you are my shelter.
   I place myself in your care.

U: *You will save me, Lord; you are a faithful God.*

1:   I will be glad and rejoice,
    because of your constant love.
      You see my suffering; you know my trouble.

2:   Be merciful to me, Lord, because I am in trouble;
      my eyes are tired from so much crying;
      I am completely worn out!
    Sorrow has shortened my life,
    and weeping has reduced my years.
      I am weak from all my troubles;
      even my bones are wasting away.

1:   All my enemies make fun of me; my neighbors scorn me;
      those who know me are afraid of me;
      when they see me in the street, they run away.
    I am forgotten by all, as though I had died;
    I am like something thrown away.

2:   *But my trust is in you, Lord; you are my God.*
    I am always in your care;
      save me from my enemies
      and from those who persecute me.
    I am your servant;
      look on me with kindness;
      save me because of your constant love!
    I call to you, Lord; don't let me be defeated!

U: *How wonderful are the good things*
      you keep for those who fear you!
    How wonderful is what you do in the sight of everyone,
    protecting those who trust you.
      You hide them in the safety of your presence.

39

L: I said, "I will be careful about what I do
    and not let my tongue make me sin;

2:   *"I will not say anything*
      while evil men are near."
    I kept quiet, not saying a word,
    not even about anything good!

1: *But my suffering only became worse,*
    and my heart was filled with anxiety.
    The more I thought, the more troubled I became;
    I could not keep from asking:
    "Lord, how long will I live? When will I die?
    Teach me how soon my life may end."

2: How short you have made my life!
    In your sight my lifetime seems nothing.
    Indeed every living man is no more than a puff of wind,
    no more than a shadow!
    All he does is for nothing;
    he gathers wealth, but doesn't know who will get it!

1: What, then, can I hope for, Lord?
    I put my hope in you.
    Save me from all my sins
    and don't let fools make fun of me.

2: *You punish a man's sins by your rebukes,*
    and like a moth, you destroy what he loves.
    Indeed a man is no more than a puff of wind!

U: *Hear my prayer, Lord, and listen to my plea;*
    don't be silent when I cry to you!

41:4

L: I said, "I have sinned against you, Lord;
    be merciful to me and cure me!"

1: My enemies say bad things about me.
    They say, "When will he die and be forgotten?"
    Those who come to see me are not sincere;
    they gather all the bad news about me,
    and then go out and tell it everywhere.

2: All who hate me whisper to each other about me,
    they imagine the worst about me.
    They say, "He is fatally ill
    and will never leave his bed again."
    Even my best friend, the one I trusted most,
    the one who shared my food, has turned against me.

U: Be merciful to me, Lord,
   and restore my health.

44

L: With our own ears we have heard it, God —

1: our ancestors have told us about it,
   about the great things you did in their time,
   in the days of long ago;
   how you yourself drove out the heathen,
   and established your people in their land;
   how you punished the other nations,
   but caused your own to prosper.

2: Your people did not conquer the land with their swords;
   they did not win it by their own power;
   it was by your power and your strength,
   by the assurance of your presence,
   showing that you loved them.

1: You are my king and my God;
   you give victory to your people.
   By your power we defeat our enemies;
   by your presence we overcome our adversaries.

2: I do not trust in my bow,
   or trust in my sword to save me;
   because you have saved us from our enemies,
   you have defeated those who hate us.

U: *We will always praise you*
   and give thanks to you forever.

1: But now, God, you have rejected us and let us be
   defeated;
   you no longer march out with our armies.
   You made us run away from our enemies,
   and they took for themselves what was ours.

2: *You allowed us to be slaughtered like sheep;*
   you scattered us in foreign countries.
   You sold your own people for a small price,
   and made no profit from the sale.

1: Our neighbors see what you did to us,
   and they mock us and make fun of us.
   You made us an object of contempt among the nations;
   they shake their heads at us in scorn.

2: *I am always in disgrace,*
   and I am covered with shame,
   from hearing the sneers and insults
   of my enemies and adversaries.

1: If we had stopped worshiping our God,
   and prayed to a foreign god,
   you would surely have discovered it,
   because you know men's secret thoughts.
   But it is for your sake
   that we are being killed all the time,
   that we are treated like sheep to be slaughtered.

2: Wake up, Lord! Why are you asleep?
   Get up! Don't reject us forever!
   Why are you hiding from us?
   Don't forget our suffering and trouble!
   We fall crushed to the ground;
   we lie defeated in the dust.

U: *Get up and help us!*
   Because of your constant love, save us!

54:1

L: Save me by your power, God;
   set me free by your might!

U: Hear my prayer, God;
   listen to my words!

L: I know that God is my helper,
   that the Lord is my defender!

U: Lord, I will gladly offer you a sacrifice;
   I will give you thanks, because you are good.

55:1

L: Hear my prayer, God;
   don't turn away from my plea!

Listen to me and answer me;
  I am worn out by my worries.
I am upset by the threats of my enemies,
by oppression from the wicked.
  They bring trouble on me;
they are angry with me and hate me.

2:   *Fear fills my heart,*
    and the terrors of death are heavy on me.
  I am gripped by fear and trembling;
    I am overcome with horror.

1: I say, "I wish I had wings like a dove!
  I would fly away and find rest!
    I would fly far away
    and make my home in the desert.
  I would hurry and find myself a shelter
  from the raging wind and the storm."

2:   *Destroy them, Lord, and confuse their speech,*
    because I see violence and riots in the city.
  Day and night they walk around the city on its walls;
    it is full of crime and trouble.
  There is destruction everywhere;
    the streets are filled with oppression and fraud.

U: Leave your troubles with the Lord,
  and he will support you;
    as for me, I will trust in God.

55:12

L: Hear my prayer, God;
    don't turn away from my plea!
  Listen to me and answer me;

1:   *I am worn out by my worries.*
    I am upset by the threats of my enemies,
    by oppression from the wicked.
2: If it were an enemy making fun of me,
  I could endure it;
    if it were an opponent boasting over me,
    I could hide myself from him.

But it is you, my companion,
my colleague and close friend!
We had intimate talks with each other,
and went with the crowd to the temple.

1: My former companion attacked his friends;
he broke his promise.
His words were smoother than cream,
but there was hatred in his heart;
his words were as soothing as oil,
but they cut like sharp swords.

2: But I call to the Lord God for help,
and he will save me.
My complaints and groans
go up to him morning, noon, and night,
and he will hear my voice.
He will bring me safely back
from the battles that I fight
against so many enemies.

U: *God, who has ruled from eternity,*
will hear me and defeat them;
there is nothing they can do about it,
because they do not fear him.

56

L: Be merciful to me, God, because I am being attacked;
my enemies persecute me all the time!

2: All day long my opponents attack me.
There are so many who fight against me.

1: When I am afraid, O Most High,
I put my trust in you.
I trust in God and praise his promise;
in him I trust, and I will not be afraid.
What can mere man do to me?

2: My enemies make trouble for me in everything I do;
they are always thinking about how to hurt me!

They gather in a hiding place
and watch everything I do, hoping to kill me.

1: *You know how troubled I am;*
you have kept a record of my tears.
Aren't they listed in your book?

2: The day I call to you,
my enemies will be turned back.
This I know — God is on my side!
I trust in God and praise his promise;
I will praise the promise of the Lord.
In him I trust, and I will not be afraid.
What can mere man do to me?

1: God, I will offer you what I have promised;
I will give you my offering of praise,
because you have rescued me from death
and kept me from defeat.
And so I walk in the presence of God,
in the light that shines on the living.

U: *When I am afraid, O Most High,*
I put my trust in you.

59:1

L: Save me from my enemies, my God;
protect me from those who attack me!
Save me from those evil men;
rescue me from those murderers!

1: Look! They are waiting to attack me;
cruel men are gathering against me.
It is not because of any sin or wrong I have done,
not because of any fault of mine, Lord,
that they hurry to their places.

2: *Rise, Lord God Almighty, and come to my help;*
see for yourself, God of Israel!

1: *They come back in the evening,*
snarling like dogs as they go about the city.
Listen to what they say!

Their tongues are like swords in their mouths,
yet they ask, "Who will hear us?"

2: *But you laugh at them, Lord;*
you make fun of all the nations!
My defender, I am protected by you;
God, you are my refuge.
My God, who loves me, will come to me;
he will let me see my enemies defeated.

1: Do not kill them, God, so that my people will not
forget.
Scatter them by your strength and destroy them,
Lord, our protector!

2: Sin is on their lips; all their words are sinful;
may they be caught in their pride!

U: *Then all people will know that God rules in Israel,*
that his rule extends over all the earth!

60:1

L: You have rejected us, God, and defeated us;
you have been angry with us — but now turn back to us!

1: You have made the land tremble, and you have cut it open;
now heal its wounds because it is about to fall apart!

2: You have made your people suffer much trouble;
you have given us wine that made us drunk.

1: You raised a banner for those who fear you,
but they turned and ran from the enemy.

U: *Save us by your might; answer our prayer,*
so that the people you love may be rescued.

61

L: Hear my cry, God; listen to my prayer!
In my despair, far from home, I call to you!

2: Take me to a safe refuge, because you are my protector,
my strong defender against my enemies.

1: *Let me live in your tent all my life;*
let me find safety under your wings.

You have heard my promises, God,
and you have given me
what belongs to those who honor you.

U: *So I will always sing praises to you,*
       as I offer you daily what I have promised.

64

L: I am in trouble, God—listen to my prayer!
    I am afraid—save me from my enemies!
2: Protect me from the plots of the wicked,
   from mobs of evil men.
    They sharpen their tongues like swords,
    and aim cruel words like arrows.
   From ambush they shoot their arrows at good men;
    they shoot suddenly, and are not afraid.
1: They encourage each other in their evil plots;
    they talk about where they will place their traps.
   "No one must see them," they say.
    They make evil plans, and say,
    "We have planned a perfect crime."
   The heart and mind of man are a mystery!
2: *But God shoots his arrows at them,*
    and suddenly they are wounded.
   He will destroy them because of their words;
    all who see them will shake their heads.
1: They will all be afraid;
    they will tell what God has done
    and think about his acts.
   All righteous people will rejoice
   because of what the Lord has done;
    they will find safety in him;
    all good people will praise him.

69:1

L: Save me, God! The water is up to my neck;
1: *I am sinking in deep mud,*

and there is no solid ground;
I am out in deep water,
and the waves are about to drown me.
I am worn out from calling for help,
and my throat is aching;
my eyes are strained from looking for your help.

2: *Those who hate me for no reason*
are more numerous than the hairs on my head;
those who lie about why they are my enemies
are strong and want to kill me.
They made me give up things I did not steal.
My sins, God, are not hidden from you;
you know how foolish I have been!
Don't let me bring shame to those who trust in you,
Lord God Almighty!
Don't let me bring disgrace to those who worship you,
God of Israel!

1: It is for your sake that I have been insulted,
and that I am covered with shame.
I am like a stranger to my brothers,
like a foreigner to my family.

2: My devotion for your temple burns in me like a fire;
the insults which are hurled at you fall on me.
I humble myself by fasting, and people insult me;
I dress myself in clothes of mourning,
and they make fun of me.
They talk about me in the streets,
and drunkards make songs about me.

1: But as for me, I will pray to you, Lord;
answer me, God, at a time you choose,
because of your great love,
because you keep your promise to save.
Save me from sinking in the mud;
keep me safe from my enemies,
and from the deep water.
Don't let the flood come over me;

don't let me drown in the depths,
or sink into the grave.

2: Answer me, Lord, in the goodness of your constant love;
   in your great compassion, turn to me!
   Don't hide yourself from your servant;
   I am in great trouble—answer me now!
   Come to me and save me;
   Rescue me from my enemies.

1: You know how I am insulted,
   how I am disgraced and dishonored;
   you see all my enemies.
   Insults have broken my heart, and I am helpless.
   I had hoped for sympathy, but there was none;
   for comfort, but I found none.

2: When I was hungry, they gave me poison;
   when I was thirsty, they offered me vinegar.
   But I am needy and in pain;
   lift me up, God, and save me!

71

L: Lord, I am safe with you;
   never let me be defeated!

2: Because you are righteous, help me and rescue me.
   Listen to me and save me!
   Be my secure shelter,
   and a strong fortress to protect me;
   you are my refuge and defense.

1: Lord, I put my hope in you;
   I have trusted in you since I was young.
   I have relied on you all my life;
   you have protected me since I was born;
   I will always praise you!

2: My life has been a mystery to many,
   but you are my strong defender.
   All day long I praise you
   and proclaim your glory.

Don't stay so far away, God;
my God, help me now!

1: I will always put my hope in you;
I will praise you more and more.
I will tell of your righteousness;
all day long I will speak of your salvation,
though it is more than I can understand.

2: I will praise your power, Lord God;
I will proclaim your righteousness, yours alone.

1: Be with me while I proclaim your power and might
to all generations to come.

2: *Your righteousness, God, reaches the skies.*
You have done great things;
there is no one like you!

1: You have sent troubles and suffering on me,
but you will restore my strength;
you will keep me from the grave.

2: You will make me greater than ever;
you will comfort me again.

1: I will indeed praise you.
I will praise your faithfulness, my God.

2: I will play hymns to you, the Holy One of Israel.

1: I will shout for joy as I play for you;

2: *with my whole being I will sing,*
because you have saved me.

72:1

L: Teach the king to judge with your righteousness, God;
share with him your own justice,
so that he will rule over your people with justice,
and govern the poor with righteousness.

U: May the land enjoy prosperity;
may it experience righteousness.
May the king judge the poor fairly;
may he help the needy
and defeat the oppressors!

73

L: God is indeed good to Israel,
to those who have pure hearts!

1: *But I was about to fall down;*
my feet were about to slip,
because I was jealous of the proud,
and I saw that the wicked are rich.

2: They do not suffer pain;
they are strong and healthy.
They don't suffer as other men do;
they don't have the troubles that others have.

1: And so they wear pride like a necklace,
and violence like a robe;
their hearts pour out evil,
and their minds are filled with wicked schemes.
They make fun of others and speak of evil things;
they are proud and talk about oppressing others.

2: They speak evil of God in heaven,
and give arrogant orders to men on earth,
so that even God's people turn to them
and eagerly believe all they say.

1: *They say, "God will not know;*
the Most High will not find out!"
This is what the wicked are like.
They have plenty and are always getting more.

2: Is it for nothing, then, that I have kept myself pure,
and my hands clean from sin?
God, you have made me suffer all day long;
every morning you have punished me!

1: If I had said such things,
I would have been untrue to your people.
So I tried hard to understand this,
even though it was so difficult,
until I went into your temple
and understood what will happen to the wicked.

2: Surely you put them in slippery places
and make them fall to destruction!
They are instantly destroyed;
they go down to a horrible end!
Lord, they are like a dream that goes away in the morning;
when you wake up you forget what they were like.

1: When my thoughts were bitter,
and my feelings were hurt,
I was stupid, and did not understand;
I acted like an animal toward you.

2: Yet I am always with you,
and you hold me by the hand.
You guide me with your advice,
and at the end you will receive me with honor.

1: What else do I have in heaven but you?
Since I have you, what else do I want on earth?
My mind and my body may grow weak,
but God is my strength;
he is all I ever want!

2: Surely those who abandon you will die,
and you will destroy those who are unfaithful to you.
But as for me, how wonderful to be near God!

U: *In the Lord God I find protection,*
to proclaim all that he has done.

74

L: Why have you abandoned us like this, God?
Will you be angry with your own people forever?

2: Remember your people,
whom you chose to be yours a long time ago,
the people you redeemed to be your own tribe.
Remember Mount Zion, where you have lived!
Come and walk over these total ruins;
our enemies have destroyed everything in the temple!

1: Your enemies shout in triumph in your meeting place;
they have taken over the temple.

They looked like woodsmen
cutting down trees with their axes.
They smashed all the wooden panels
with their axes and battering rams.

2: *They set your temple on fire;*
they profaned the place where you are worshiped;
they wrecked it all.
They decided to crush us completely;
they burned down every holy place in the land.

1: All our sacred symbols are gone;
there are no prophets left,
and no one knows how long this will last.

2: How long, God, will our enemies make fun of us?
Will they insult your name forever?
Why have you refused to help us?
Why do you keep your hands behind you?

1: But God, you have been our king from the beginning;
you win victories on earth.
With your mighty strength you divided the sea
and smashed the heads of the sea monsters;

2: *you made springs and fountains flow;*
you dried up the rivers.
You created the day and the night;
you set the sun and the moon in their places;
you set the limits of the earth;
you made summer and winter.

1: But remember, Lord, that your enemies make fun of you;
that they are foolish and despise you.
Don't abandon your helpless people to their cruel enemies;
don't forget your persecuted people!

2: Remember the covenant you made with us.
There is violence in every dark corner of the land!
Don't let the oppressed be defeated,
but let the poor and needy praise you.

1: Rise, God, and defend your cause!

Remember that the godless make fun of you
all day long!
Don't forget the angry shouts of your enemies, ·
the continuous noise made by your foes.

77

L: I cry aloud to God;
I cry aloud, and he hears me.

1: In time of trouble I pray to the Lord;
all night long I lift my hands in prayer,
but I cannot find comfort.
I think of God, and I sigh;
I meditate, and I feel discouraged.

2: He doesn't let me sleep;
I am so worried that I cannot speak.
I think of days gone by and remember years of long ago.
I spend the night in deep thought;
I meditate, and this is what I ask myself:

1: *"Will the Lord always reject me?*
Will he never again be pleased with me?
Has he stopped loving me?
Is his promise no longer good?
Has God forgotten to be merciful?
Has anger taken the place of his compassion?"

2: Then I said, "What hurts me most is this—
that God is no longer powerful."

1: *I will remember your great acts, Lord;*
I will recall the wonders you did in the past.

2: I will think about all that you have done;
I will meditate on all your deeds.

1: Everything you do, God, is holy!
No god is as great as you!
You are the God who works miracles;
you showed your might among the nations.
By your power you saved your people,
the descendants of Jacob and of Joseph.

2: *When the waters saw you, God, they were afraid,*
   and the depths of the sea trembled.
   The clouds poured down rain;
   thunder crashed from the sky,
   and lightning flashed in all directions.
   The crash of your thunder rolled out,
   and flashes of lightning lit up the whole world;
   the earth trembled and shook.
   You walked through the sea;
   you crossed the deep ocean,
   but your footprints could not be seen.

U: *You led your people like a shepherd.*

79

L: God, the heathen have invaded your people's land!

1: *They have profaned your holy temple*
   and left Jerusalem in ruins.
   They left the bodies of your people for birds to eat,
   the bodies of your servants for wild animals.

2: *They shed your people's blood like water;*
   blood flowed like water all over Jerusalem,
   and no one was left to bury the corpses.
   The nations around us make fun of us;
   they laugh at us and mock us.

1: How long will you be angry with us, Lord? Forever?
   Will your anger continue to burn like fire?
   Be angry with the nations that do not worship you,
   with the people who reject you!
   They have killed our people and ruined our country.

2: Do not punish us for the sins of our ancestors,
   but have mercy on us now,
   because we have lost all hope.

1: Help us, God our Savior,
   for the sake of your own honor;
   rescue us and forgive our sins,
   so that people will praise you.

2: Listen to the groans of the prisoners,
and by your great power
free those who are condemned to die.

U: *We, your people, the sheep of your flock,*
will thank you forever
and praise you for all time to come.

80

L: Listen to us, Shepherd of Israel;
hear us, leader of your flock.

1: Seated on your throne on the cherubim, reveal your love.
Show us your strength; come and save us!

2: Bring us back, God!
Show us your love, and we will be saved!

1: How much longer, Lord God Almighty,
will you be angry with your people's prayers?
You have given us tears to eat,
and a large cup of tears to drink.
You let the neighboring nations fight over our land,
and our enemies make fun of us.

2:   *Bring us back, Almighty God!*
Show us your love, and we will be saved!

1: You brought a grapevine out of Egypt;
you drove out other nations
and planted it in their land.
You cleared a place for it to grow;
its roots went deep,
and it spread out over the whole land.
It covered the hills with its shade,
the giant cedars with its branches.

2:   *Why did you break down the fences around it?*
Now any passing by can steal its grapes;
wild pigs trample it down,
and all the wild animals eat it.

1: Turn to us, Almighty God!

> *Look down from heaven at us;*
> *come and save your grapevine!*
> Come and save this vine that you yourself planted,
> this young vine you made grow so strong!

2: *Our enemies have set it on fire and cut it down;*
   protect and preserve the people you have chosen,
   the nation you made grow so strong!

U: *We will never turn away from you again;*
   keep us alive, and we will praise you.
   Bring us back, Lord God Almighty!
   Show us your love, and we will be saved!

83:1

L: God, don't keep silent;
   don't be still, God, don't be quiet!

1: Look! Your enemies are in revolt,
   and those who hate you are rebelling.
   They are making secret plans against your people;
   they are plotting against those you protect.
   "Come," they say, "let us destroy their nation,
   so that Israel will be forgotten forever!"

2: My God, scatter them like dust,
   like straw blown away by the wind.
   As the fire burns the forest,
   as the flames set the hills on fire,
   so chase them away with your storm
   and terrify them with your fierce winds.
   Cover their faces with shame, Lord,
   so they will want to serve you.

U: *May they know that only you are the Lord,*
   supreme ruler over all the earth!

85:4

L: Bring us back, God our Savior,
   and stop being displeased with us!

1: *Will you be angry with us forever?*
   Will your anger never cease?

2: Please renew our strength,
and we, your people, will praise you.
Show us your constant love, Lord,
and give us your saving help.

1: I am listening to what the Lord God is saying;
he promises peace to us, his own people,
if we do not go back to our foolish ways.

2: Surely he is ready to save those who honor him,
and his saving presence will remain in our land.

U: *Love and faithfulness will come together;*
righteousness and peace will meet.
Man's loyalty will reach up from the earth,
and God's righteousness will look down from heaven.

86

L: Listen to me, Lord, and answer me,
because I am weak and helpless.

1: *Save me from death, because I am loyal to you;*
save me, because I am your servant and trust in you.

2: *You are my God, so be merciful to me, Lord;*
I pray to you all day long.
Make your servant glad, Lord,
because my prayers go up to you.
Lord, you are good and forgiving,
full of constant love for all who pray to you.

1: Listen, Lord, to my prayer;
hear my cries for help.
I call to you in times of trouble,
because you answer my prayer.

2: There is no other god like you, Lord,
not one who can do what you can do.
All nations you have created
will come and bow down to you.
They will praise your greatness,
because only you, God, are mighty;
only you do wonderful things.

1: Teach me, Lord, what you want me to do,
   and I will obey you faithfully;
      teach me to serve you with complete devotion.

2: I will praise you with all my heart, Lord my God;
      I will proclaim your greatness forever.
   How great is your constant love for me!
      You have saved me from the depths of the grave.

1: God, arrogant men are coming against me;
      cruel men are trying to kill me,
      people who pay no attention to you.

U: Lord, you are a merciful and loving God,
   slow to anger, always kind and faithful.
      Turn to me and have mercy on me;
      strengthen me and save me.

88

L: Lord God, my Savior, I cry out all day,
   and at night I come before you.

1:    *Hear my prayer; listen to my cry for help!*
   So many troubles have fallen on me
   that I am close to death.
      I am like all others who are about to die;
      all my strength is gone.
   I am abandoned among the dead;
      I am like the slain lying in their graves.

2: You have thrown me into the depths of the tomb,
   into the darkest and deepest pit.
      Your anger lies heavy on me,
      and I am crushed beneath its waves.

1: You have caused my friends to abandon me;
      you have made me repulsive to them.
   I am closed in and cannot escape;
   my eyes are weak from suffering.
      Lord, every day I call to you,
      and lift my hands to you in prayer!

2: Lord, I call to you for help;

every morning I pray to you.
Why do you reject me, Lord?
Why do you hide yourself from me?

1: Ever since I was young
I have suffered and been near death;
I am worn out from the burden of your punishments.
Your furious anger rolls over me;
your terrible attacks destroy me.
All day long they surround me like a flood;
they close in on me from all sides.

2: You have made even my closest friends abandon me;
darkness is the only companion I have left.

U: Hear my prayer;
listen to my cry for help!

90

L: Lord, you have always been our home.

2: *Before the hills were created,*
before you brought the world into being,
you are eternally God, without beginning or end.

1: You tell men to return to what they were;
you change them back to soil.
A thousand years to you are like one day;
they are like yesterday, already gone,
like a short hour in the night.

2: You carry men away like a flood;
they last no longer than a dream.
They are like weeds that sprout in the morning,
that grow and burst into bloom,
then dry up and die in the evening.

1: We are destroyed by your anger;
we are terrified by your fury.
You place our sins before you,
our secret sins where you can see them.

2: Our lifetime is cut short by your anger;
our life comes to an end like a whisper.

Seventy years is all we have —
eighty years, if we are strong;
   yet all they bring us is worry and trouble;
   life is soon over, and we are gone.

1: Who really knows the full power of your anger?
Who knows what fear your fury can bring?
   Teach us how short our life is,
   so that we may become wise.

2: How long, Lord, before you relent?
Have pity on your servants!
   Fill us each morning with your constant love,
   that we may sing and be glad all our life.
Give us now as much happiness as you gave us sadness,
during all those years when we had troubles.

1: *Let us, your servants, see your mighty acts;*
let our descendants see your glorious might.

U: *Lord our God, may your blessings be with us,*
   and give us success in all we do!

94

L: Lord, you are a God who punishes;
   reveal your anger!

1: You are the judge of all men;
rise and give the proud what they deserve!

2: *How much longer will the wicked be glad?*
   How much longer, Lord?
How much longer will evildoers be proud
and boast about their crimes?

1: *They crush your people, Lord;*
   they oppress those who belong to you.
They kill widows and orphans,
and murder the strangers who live in our land.

2: *They say, "The Lord doesn't see us;*
   the God of Israel does not notice!"

1: My people, how can you be such stupid fools?
When will you ever learn?

God made our ears — can't he hear?
He made our eyes — can't he see?

2: He is in charge of the nations — won't he punish them?
 He is the teacher of all men — doesn't he know?
The Lord knows what they think;
 he knows how senseless their reasoning is.

1: Lord, happy is the man whom you instruct,
the man to whom you teach your law,
 to give him rest from days of trouble,
 until a grave is dug for the wicked.

2: The Lord will not abandon his people;
 he will not desert those who belong to him.

1: Justice will again be found in courts of judgment,
 and all righteous people will support it.

2: Who stood up for me against the wicked?
Who took my side against the evildoers?

1: *If the Lord had not helped me,*
 I would have gone quickly to the land of silence.

2: I said, "I am falling";
but, Lord, your constant love held me up.

U: *When I am anxious and worried,*
 you comfort me and make me glad.

L: You have nothing to do with corrupt judges,
who make injustice legal,
who plot against good men,
and sentence the innocent to death.

U: *But the Lord defends me; my God protects me.*

101 – 102

L: My song is about loyalty and justice,
and I sing it to you, Lord.
 When will you come to me?

1: I will live a pure life in my house;
 I will never tolerate evil.

2: Listen to my prayer, Lord,
   and hear my cry for help!
   Don't hide yourself from me when I am in trouble!
   Listen to me, and answer me quickly when I call!

1: My life disappears like smoke;
   my body burns like fire.
   I am beaten down like dry grass;
   I have lost my desire for food.
   I groan aloud;
   I am nothing but skin and bones.

2: I am like a wild bird in the desert,
   like an owl in abandoned ruins.
   I lie awake; I am like a lonely bird on a housetop.
   All day long my enemies insult me;
   those who make fun of me use my name in cursing.

1: Ashes are my food,
   and my tears are mixed with my drink,
   because of your anger and fury.
   You picked me up and threw me away.
   My life is like the evening shadows;
   I am like dry grass.

2: But you, Lord, are king forever;
   all generations will remember you.
   You will rise and take pity on Zion;
   the time has come to have mercy on her;
   this is the right time!
   Your servants love her, even though she is destroyed.
   they have pity on her, even though she is in ruins.

1: The nations will fear the Lord;
   all the kings of the earth will fear his power.
   When the Lord rebuilds Zion,
   he will reveal his greatness.
   He will hear his abandoned people
   and listen to their prayer.

2: Write down for the coming generation what the Lord did,
   so that people not yet born will praise him.

U: The Lord looked down from his holy place on high,
   he looked down from heaven to the earth,
   to hear the groans of prisoners,
   and to set free those who were condemned to die.
And so men will proclaim the name of the Lord in Zion;
   they will give thanks to him in Jerusalem,
   when nations and kingdoms come together
   and worship the Lord.

1: The Lord made me weak while I was still young;
   he has shortened my life.
   My God, do not take me away now,
   before I grow old!

2: Lord, you live forever;
   long ago you created the earth,
   and with your own hands you made the heavens.
They will all disappear, but you will remain;
   they will all wear out like clothes.
You will change them like clothes, and they will vanish;
but you are always the same, and your life never ends.

U: *Our children will live in safety,*
   and their descendants will always live
   under your protection.

109:1

L: I praise you, God; don't be silent!

1: *Wicked men and liars have attacked me,*
   telling lies about me.
They say terrible things about me,
attacking me for no reason.
   They oppose me, even though I love them
   and have prayed for them.
They pay me back evil for good,
and hatred for love.

2: *Lord, my God, help me as you have promised,*
   and rescue me because of the goodness of your love.
I am poor and needy;
   I am hurt to the depths of my heart.

I am about to vanish like an evening shadow;
I am blown away like an insect.
My knees are weak from lack of food;
my body is thin and feeble.
When people see me, they make fun of me;
they shake their heads in scorn.

L: Help me, Lord my God;
save me because of your constant love!

U: I will give loud thanks to the Lord;
I will praise him in the meeting of the people,
because he defends the poor man,
to save him from those who condemn him to death.

119:49

L: Remember your promise to me, your servant;
it has given me hope.

1: *Even in my suffering I was comforted,*
because your promise gave me life.
The proud have been scornful of me,
but I have not departed from your law.

2: *I remember the instructions you gave me in the past,*
and they bring me comfort, Lord.

1: I am filled with anger,
when I see the wicked breaking your law.
Living far from my real home,
I compose songs about your commands.

2: In the night I think of you, Lord, and I obey your law.
This is my happiness: I obey your commands.

1: You are all I want, Lord; I promise to obey your laws.

2: *I ask you with all my heart:*
have mercy on me, as you have promised!

1: I have considered my conduct,
and promise to follow your rules.
Without delay, I hurry to obey your commandments.

2: The wicked draw their ropes tight around me,
but I do not forget your law.

In the middle of the night I wake up
to praise you for your righteous judgments.
I am a friend of all who serve you,
of all who obey your laws.

U: *Lord, the earth is full of your constant love;*
     teach me your commandments!

119:81

L: I am worn out, Lord, waiting for you to save me;
   I place my trust in your word.

1: My eyes are tired from watching for what you promised,
   while I ask, "When will you help me?"

2:   *I am as useless as a discarded wineskin;*
     yet I have not forgotten your commands.

1: How much longer do I have to wait?
   Proud men, who do not obey your law,
   have dug pits to catch me.
   Men persecute me with lies; help me!

2: They have almost succeeded in killing me,
   but I have not neglected your rules;
   your commandments are all trustworthy.

U: *Because of your constant love, be good to me,*
     so that I may obey your laws.

119:145

L: With all my heart I call to you;

2:   *answer me, Lord, and I will obey your commands!*
   I call to you;
     save me, and I will follow your rules!

1: Before sunrise I call to you for help;
   I place my hope in your promise.

2: All night long I lie awake,
   to meditate on your instructions.
     Hear me, Lord, according to your constant love;
   preserve my life, according to your goodness!

1: *You are near to me, Lord,*
   and all your promises are true.
   Long ago I learned about your instructions;
   you made them to last forever.

U: With all my heart I call to you;
   . *answer me, Lord.*

119:169

L: Let my cry for help reach you, Lord!
   Give me understanding, as you have promised.

1: Let my prayer come before you,
   and save me, according to your promise!
   I will always praise you,
   because you teach me your rules.

2: *I will sing about your law,*
   because your commands are just.
   Be always ready to help me,
   because I follow your commands.

1: *How I long for your salvation, Lord!*
   I find happiness in your law.
   Give me life, so that I may praise you;
   may your instructions help me!

2: *I wander about like a lost sheep;*
   so come and look for me, your servant.

123

L: Lord, I look up to you,
   up to heaven, where you rule.

1: *As the servant depends on his master,*
   and the maid depends on her mistress,
   so we keep looking to you, Lord our God,
   until you have mercy on us.

2: Be merciful to us, Lord, be merciful;
   we have been treated with so much contempt!
   We have been mocked too long by the rich,
   and scorned by proud oppressors!

L: Lord, I look up to you;

U: *Be merciful, Lord, be merciful.*

129 – 130

L: Israel, tell how cruelly your enemies have persecuted you
ever since you were young!

1: *"Ever since I was young,*
my enemies have persecuted me cruelly,
but they have not overcome me.
They cut deep wounds in my back,
and made it like a plowed field.
But the Lord, the righteous one,
has freed me from slavery."

2: May all who hate Zion be defeated and driven back!
May they be like grass growing on the housetops,
that dries up before it can be cut.
No one gathers it up, or carries it away in bundles.
No one who passes by will say,
"May the Lord bless you!
We bless you in the name of the Lord!"

1: In my despair I call to you, Lord.
Hear my cry, Lord, listen to my call for help!
If you kept a record of our sins,
who could escape being condemned?
But you forgive us, so that we should fear you.

2: I wait eagerly for the Lord's help,
and in his word I trust.
I wait for the Lord,
more eagerly than watchmen wait for the dawn.

L: Israel, trust in the Lord,
because his love is constant,
and he is always willing to save.

U: *He will save his people Israel from all their sins.*

139

L: Lord, you have examined me, and you know me.

1: *You know everything I do;*
from far away you understand all my thoughts.
You see me, whether I am working or resting;
you know all my actions.

2: *Even before I speak you already know what I will say.*
You are all around me, on every side;
you protect me with your power.
Your knowledge of me is overwhelming;
it is too deep for me to understand.

1: Where could I go to escape from your Spirit?
Where could I get away from your presence?

2: If I went up to heaven, you would be there;
if I lay down in the world of the dead,
you would be there.
If I flew away beyond the east,
or lived in the farthest place in the west,
you would be there to lead me,
you would be there to help me.

1: I could ask the darkness to hide me,
or the light around me to turn into night,
but even the darkness is not dark for you,
and the night is as bright as the day.
Darkness and light are the same to you.

2: You created every part of me;
you put me together in my mother's womb.
I praise you because you are to be feared;
all you do is strange and wonderful.
I know it with all my heart.
You saw my bones being formed,
carefully put together in my mother's womb,
when I was growing there in secret.
You saw me before I was born.
The days that had been created for me
had all been recorded in your book,
before any of them had ever begun.

1: *God, how difficult your thoughts are for me;*
how many of them there are!

If I counted them,
they would be more than the grains of sand.
When I awake, I am still with you.

2: Examine me, God, and know my mind;
   test me, and discover my thoughts.
   Find out if there is any deceit in me,
   and guide me in the eternal way.

140:1

L: Save me, Lord, from evil men;
   keep me safe from violent men.

2: They are always plotting evil,
   always stirring up quarrels.
   *Their tongues are like deadly snakes,
   their words are like a cobra's poison.*

1: Protect me, Lord, from the power of the wicked;
   keep me safe from violent men, who plot my downfall.
   Proud men have laid a trap for me;
   *they have spread a net of ropes,
   and along the path they have set traps to catch me.*

2: I say to the Lord, "You are my God."
   Hear my cry for help, Lord!
   Lord, my God, my strong Savior,
   you have protected me in battle.

1: *I know that you, Lord, defend the cause of the poor,
   and the rights of the needy.*
   The righteous will praise you indeed;
   they will live in your presence.

U: Save me, Lord!
   Hear my cry for help!

141

L: I call to you, Lord; help me now!
   Listen to me when I call to you.
   Receive my prayer as incense,
   my uplifted hands as an evening sacrifice.

1: *Lord, place a guard at my mouth,*
    a sentry at the door of my lips.
    Keep me from wanting to do wrong,
    or to join evil men in their wickedness.
    May I never take part in their feasts!

2: A good man may punish me
    and reprimand me in kindness,
    but I will not let an evil man anoint my head,
    because I am always praying against his evil deeds.

1: *But I, Lord God, keep trusting in you;*
    I seek your protection; don't let me die!

2: Protect me from the traps they have set for me,
    from the snares of those evildoers.
    May the wicked fall into their own traps,
    while I go by unharmed.

142

L: I call to the Lord for help;
    I plead with him.

2: I bring him all my complaints;
    I tell him all my troubles.
    When I am ready to give up,
    he knows what I should do.

1: *In the path where I walk*
    my enemies have hidden a trap for me.
    I look beside me and I see
    that there is no one to help me;
    there is no one to protect me; no one cares for me.

2: Lord, I cry to you for help;
    you, Lord, are my protector;
    you are all I want in this life.
    Listen to my cry for help,
    because I am sunk in despair.
    Save me from my enemies,
    who are much stronger than I am.

1: Rescue me from my trouble;

then in the meeting of your people I will praise you,
because you have been good to me.

143

L: Lord, hear my prayer, listen to my plea!

2: *You are righteous and faithful, so answer me!*
Don't put me, your servant, on trial;
  no one is innocent in your sight.

1: My enemy has persecuted me,
and completely defeated me.
  He has put me in a dark prison,
  and I am like those who died long ago.
So I am ready to give up;
  I am in deep despair.

2: I remember the days gone by;
  I think about all that you have done,
  I bring to mind all your deeds.
I lift up my hands to you in prayer;
  like dry ground my soul thirsts for you.

1: Answer me now, Lord!
  I have lost all hope!
Don't hide yourself from me,
or I will be among those who go down
to the land of the dead.

2: *I trust in you;*
  in the morning remind me of your constant love.
My prayers go up to you;
  show me the way I should go.

1: I go to you for protection, Lord;
  rescue me from my enemies.
You are my God; teach me to do your will.
  May your Spirit be good to me
  and guide me on a safe path.

U: Save me, Lord, as you have promised;
  in your goodness, rescue me from my troubles!

144

L: Praise the Lord, my protector;
> *he trains me for battle, and prepares me for war.*
He is my protector and defender,
> *he is my shelter and Savior,*
> *in whom I trust for safety.*

1: Lord, what is man, that you notice him;
mere man, that you pay attention to him?
> *He is like a puff of wind;*
> *his days are like a passing shadow.*

2: Lord, pull back the sky and come down;
> *touch the mountains, and they will pour out smoke.*
Send flashes of lightning and scatter your enemies;
> *shoot your arrows and send them running!*
Reach down from above,
> *pull me out of the deep water and save me.*

1: I will sing you a new song, God;
I will play the harp and sing to you.
> *You give victory to kings,*
> *and rescue your servant David.*

2: May our sons in their youth
be like plants that grow up strong.
> *May our daughters be like statues,*
> *which adorn the corners of a palace.*

1: May our barns be filled with crops of every kind.
> *May the sheep in our fields*
> *bear young by the tens of thousands.*
May our cattle reproduce plentifully,
without miscarriage or loss.
> *May there be no cries of distress in our streets!*

U: Happy is the nation of whom this is true;
> *Happy are the people whose God is the Lord!*

PSALMS OF AFFIRMATION

18:1

L: How I love you, Lord!
You are my defender.

1: The Lord is my Savior;
he is my strong fortress.
My God is my protection,
and I am safe with him.
He protects me like a shield;
he defends me and keeps me safe.
I call to the Lord, and he saves me from my enemies.
Praise the Lord!

2: Death pulled its ropes tight around me;
the waves of destruction rolled over me.
Death pulled its ropes tight around me;
the grave set its trap for me.
In my trouble I called to the Lord;
I called to my God for help.
In his temple he heard my voice;
my cry for help reached his ears.

20

L: May the Lord answer you in the day of trouble!
May the God of Jacob protect you!

1: May he send you help from his temple
and give you aid from Mount Zion!
*May he accept all your offerings
and be pleased with all your sacrifices.*
May he give you what you desire
and make all your plans succeed.

2: *Then we will shout for joy over your victory*
    and celebrate by praising our God.
    May the Lord answer all your requests!

1: *Now I know that the Lord gives victory*
    to his chosen king;
    he answers him from his holy heaven,
    and by his great power makes him victorious.

2: Some trust in their war chariots,
    and others in their horses,
    but we trust in the power of the Lord our God!
    They will stumble and fall,
    but we will rise and stand firm!

L: Give victory to the king, Lord;

U: *the Lord will answer us when we call.*

21:1

L: The king is glad, Lord, because you gave him strength;
    he is full of joy, because you made him victorious.
    You have given him what he wanted;
    you have answered his request.

1: You came to him with great blessings
    and set a gold crown on his head.
    He asked for life, and you gave it;
    a long and lasting life.

2: His glory is great because of your help;
    you have given him fame and majesty.
    Your blessings are upon him forever,
    your presence fills him with gladness.

L: The king trusts in the Most High;
    and because of the Lord's constant love
    he will be king forever.

U: Come, Lord, with your strength!
    We will sing and praise your power.

23

L: The Lord is my shepherd;
    I have everything I need.

1: He lets me rest in fields of green grass;
   he leads me to quiet pools of fresh water.

2: He gives me new strength.
   He guides me in the right way, as he has promised.

1: Even if that way goes through deepest darkness,
   I will not be afraid, Lord, because you are with me!
   Your shepherd's rod and staff keep me safe.

2: *You prepare a banquet for me,*
   where all my enemies can see me;
   you welcome me by pouring ointment on my head
   and filling my cup to the brim.

U: *Certainly your goodness and love will be with me*
   as long as I live;
   and your house will be my home forever.

27:1

L: The Lord is my light and my salvation;
   I will fear no one.
   The Lord protects me from all danger;
   I will not be afraid.

1: When evil men attack me and try to kill me,
   they stumble and fall.
   Even if a whole army surrounds me,
   I will not be afraid;
   even if my enemies attack me, I will still trust God.

2: *I have asked the Lord for one thing;*
   one thing only do I want:
   to live in the Lord's house all my life,
   to marvel at his goodness,
   and to ask his guidance there.

1: *In times of trouble he will protect me in his shelter;*
   he will keep me safe in his temple,
   and place me securely on a high rock.

2: *So I will triumph over my enemies around me.*
   With shouts of joy I will offer sacrifices in his temple;

U: *I will sing, I will praise the Lord!*

34

L: I will always thank the Lord;
   I will never stop praising him.

2: I will praise him for what he has done;
   may all who are oppressed listen and be glad!
   Proclaim with me the Lord's greatness;
   let us praise his name together!

1: I prayed to the Lord and he answered me;
   he freed me from all my fears.
   The oppressed look to him and are glad;
   they will never be disappointed.
   The helpless call to him, and he answers;
   he saves them from all their troubles.
   His angel guards those who fear the Lord
   and rescues them from danger.

2: Find out for yourself how good the Lord is!
   Happy is the man who finds safety with him!

1: Fear the Lord, all his people;
   those who fear him have all they need.
   Even lions lack food and go hungry,
   but those who obey the Lord lack nothing good.

L: Come, my young friends, and listen to me;
   I will teach you to fear the Lord.

2: *Would you like to enjoy life?*
   Do you want long life and happiness?
   Then keep from speaking evil and from telling lies.
   Turn away from evil and do good;
   desire peace and do your best to have it.

1: The Lord watches over the righteous
   and listens to their cries;
   but he opposes those who do evil,
   so that even their own people forget them.

2: Righteous men call to the Lord and he listens;
   he rescues them from all their troubles.
   The Lord is near to those who are discouraged;
   he saves those who have lost all hope.

1: The good man suffers many troubles,
   but the Lord saves him from them all;
   the Lord preserves him completely;
   not one of his bones is broken.

U: The Lord will save his servants;
   those who go to him for protection will be spared.

78:1

L: Listen, my people, to my teaching,
   and pay attention to what I say.
   I am going to speak to you,
   and tell you mysteries from the past,
   things we have heard and known,
   that our ancestors have told us.

1: *We will not keep them from our children,*
   but will tell the next generation
   about the Lord's power and his mighty acts,
   and the wonderful things that he has done.

2: He gave laws to the people of Israel,
   and commandments to the descendants of Jacob.
   He gave orders to our ancestors
   to teach his laws to their children,
   so that the next generation might learn them,
   and in turn should tell their children.

1: In this way they also would put their trust in God,
   and not forget what he has done,
   but always obey his commandments.
   They should not be like their ancestors,
   a rebellious and disobedient people,
   whose trust in God was never firm,
   and who did not remain faithful to him.

2: They did not keep their covenant with God;
   they refused to obey his law.
   They forgot what he had done,
   the miracles that he had shown them.

1: While their ancestors watched, God performed a miracle

in the land of Egypt.
He divided the sea and led them through;
he made the waters stand like walls.

2: By day he led them with a cloud,
and all night long with the light of a fire.
He split rocks open in the desert,
and gave them water from the depths.
He caused a stream to come out of the rock,
and made the water flow like a river.

1: *But they continued to sin against God,*
and rebelled in the desert against the Most High.
They deliberately put God to the test,
by demanding the food they wanted.

2: *They spoke against God, saying,*
"Can God set a table in the desert?
It is true that he struck the rock,
and water flowed out in a torrent;
but can he also provide us with bread,
and give his people meat?"

1: *And so the Lord was angry when he heard them;*
he attacked his people with fire,
and his anger against them grew,
because they had no faith in him
and didn't believe that he would save them.

2: *But he spoke to the sky above,*
and commanded its doors to open;
he gave them grain from heaven,
by sending down manna for them to eat.
So they ate the food of angels.
God gave them all they could eat.

1: Then he caused the east wind to blow,
and by his power he stirred up the south wind,
and sent down birds on them as thick as dust,
as many as the grains of sand on the shore;
they fell in the middle of the camp,
all around the tents.

2: *So the people ate and were satisfied;*
God gave them all they wanted.
But while they were still eating,
even before they had satisfied themselves,
God became angry with them,
and killed the strongest men,
the best young men of Israel!

1: *In spite of all his miracles the people kept on sinning,*
and would not believe;
so he ended their days like a breath,
their lives with sudden disaster.
But when he would kill some of them,
the rest would turn to him;
they would repent and pray earnestly to him.
They remembered that God was their protector,
that the Most High was their Savior.

2: But their words were all lies,
and everything they said was flattery.
They were not loyal to him;
they were not faithful to their covenant with him.

1: But God was merciful to his people.
He forgave their sin and did not destroy them.
Many times he kept from being angry
and restrained his fury.
He remembered that they were only men,
and like a wind that blows by and is gone.

78:38

L: God was merciful to his people.
He forgave their sin and did not destroy them.
Many times he kept from being angry
and restrained his fury.
He remembered that they were only men,
and like a wind that blows by and is gone.

2: How often they rebelled against him in the desert;
how many times they made him sad!
Again and again they put God to the test,
and made the Holy One of Israel angry.

1:   *They forgot his great power;*
they forgot the time he saved them from their enemies,
and performed his mighty acts and miracles
in the land of Egypt.

2:   *He turned the rivers into blood,*
  so that the Egyptians couldn't drink from their streams.
He sent flies among them, that tormented them,
and frogs, that ruined their fields.
  He sent caterpillars to eat their crops,
  and grasshoppers to destroy their fields.
He killed their grapevines with hail,
and their fig trees with frost.
  He killed their cattle with hail,
  and their flocks with lightning.

1: He blasted them with his furious anger and fierce rage;
  he caused them great distress
  by sending the destroying angels.
He did not restrain his anger, or spare their lives,
but killed them with a plague.
  He killed the firstborn sons
  of all the families in Egypt.

2: Then he led his people out like a shepherd;
  he guided them through the desert.
He led them safely, and they were not afraid;
but the sea covered their enemies.
  He brought them to his holy land,
  to the mountains which he himself conquered.

1: He drove out the inhabitants as his people advanced;
  he divided the land among the tribes of Israel,
  and there let them settle in their tents.

2: But they rebelled against Almighty God,
and put him to the test.
  They did not obey his commandments,
  but were rebellious and disloyal like their ancestors,
  unreliable as arrows shot from a crooked bow.
They angered him with their heathen places of worship,
and made him jealous with their idols.

1:   *God was angry when he saw it,*
   and so rejected his people completely.
He abandoned his tent in Shiloh,
the home where he had lived among men.
   He allowed the enemies to capture the covenant box,
   where his power and glory were seen.
He was angry with his own people,
and let them be killed by their enemies.
   Young men were killed in war,
   and young women had no one to marry.
Priests were killed by swords,
and their widows could not mourn for them.

2:   *At last the Lord woke up as though from sleep;*
   he was like a strong man excited by wine.
He drove his enemies back, in lasting and shameful defeat.
   He rejected the descendants of Joseph;
   he did not select the tribe of Ephraim.

1: Instead he chose the tribe of Judah,
and Mount Zion, which he dearly loves.
   There he built his temple, like his home in heaven;
he made it firm like the earth, secure for all time.

2: *He chose his servant David;*
he took him from taking care of the sheep
and looking after the lambs.
   He made him king of Israel,
   the shepherd of the people of God.

91

1: Whoever goes to the Most High for safety,
whoever remains under the protection of the Almighty,
can say to the Lord,
   "You are my defender and protector!
   You are my God; in you I trust."

2: He will surely keep you safe from all hidden dangers,
and from all deadly diseases.
   He will cover you with his wings;
you will be safe under his care;
   his faithfulness will protect and defend you.

1: You will not be afraid of dangers at night,
   or of sudden attacks during the day,
   of the plagues that strike in the dark,
   or of the evils that kill in daylight.
   A thousand may fall beside you,
   ten thousand all around you,
   but you will not be harmed.

2: Because you made the Lord your defender,
   the Most High your protector,
   no disaster will strike you,
   no violence will come near your home.

1: *God will put his angels in charge of you,*
   to protect you wherever you go.
   They will hold you up with their hands,
   to keep you from hurting your feet on the rocks.
   You will trample down lions and snakes,
   fierce lions and poisonous snakes.

2: God says, "I will save those who love me,
   and protect those who know me.
   When they call to me, I will answer them;
   when they are in trouble, I will be with them.
   I will rescue them and honor them.
   I will surely save them."

105

L: Give thanks to the Lord,
   proclaim his greatness,
   and make known to the nations what he has done!

1: Sing to him, sing praise to him;
   tell all the wonderful things he has done!
   Be glad that we belong to him;
   let all who serve the Lord rejoice!

2: Go to the Lord for help;
   stay in his presence always.
   You descendants of Jacob, his chosen one;
   remember his great and wonderful miracles,
   and the judgments he gave.

1: He, the Lord, is our God;
  his commands are for all the world.
He will keep his covenant forever,
  his promises for a thousand generations.
The Lord made an eternal covenant with Israel,
a lasting agreement with Jacob.

2: *God's people were few in number,*
    and they were strangers in the land.
When the Lord sent famine to their country,
and took away all their food,
he sent Joseph ahead of them,
who had been sold as a slave.
    His feet were hurt by tight chains,
    and an iron collar was put around his neck,
    until what he had predicted came true.
The word of the Lord proved him right.

1: *Then the king of Egypt had him released;*
    the ruler of nations set him free.
He put him in charge of his government,
and made him ruler over all the land,
with complete authority over the king's officials,
and power to instruct his advisers.

2: *Then Jacob went to Egypt,*
    and settled in that country.
The Lord let his people have many children,
and made them stronger than their enemies.
    He made the Egyptians hate his people,
    and act deceitfully with his servants.

1: Then he sent his servant Moses,
and Aaron, whom he chose.
    They did God's mighty acts,
    and performed miracles in Egypt.
He sent darkness on the land,
but the Egyptians did not obey his command.
    He turned their rivers into blood,
    and killed all their fish.
Their country was filled with frogs, even the king's palace.

2:    *God commanded, and flies and gnats*
      filled the whole country.
He sent hail and lightning on their land,
instead of rain;
    he destroyed their grapevines and fig trees,
    and broke down the trees.
He commanded, and the grasshoppers came,
countless millions of them;
    they ate all the plants in the land;
    they ate all the crops.
He killed the firstborn sons
of all the families of Egypt.

1:    *Then he led the Israelites out;*
    they carried silver and gold,
    and all of them were strong and healthy.
The Egyptians were glad when they left,
because they were afraid of them.

2:    *He put a cloud over his people*
    and a fire to give them light by night.
They asked, and he sent quails,
    he gave them food from heaven to satisfy them.

1: He opened a rock, and water gushed out,
    flowing through the desert like a river.
    He remembered his sacred promise
    to Abraham his servant.

2: So he led his people out with singing,
    his chosen people with shouts of joy.

U: *Praise the Lord!*

106:1

L: Praise the Lord!

1:    *Give thanks to the Lord, because he is good;*
    his love is eternal.

2: Who can tell all the great things he has done?
    Who can praise him enough?

U: *Happy are those who obey his command,*
    who always do what is right!

L: Remember me, Lord, when you help your people;
    include me, when you save them.
    Let me see the prosperity of your people.
    Let me share in the happiness of your nation,
    in the glad pride of those who belong to you.

2: We have sinned, as our ancestors did;
    we have been wicked and evil.
    Our ancestors in Egypt did not understand
    God's wonderful acts;
    they forgot the many times he showed his love for them,
    and they rebelled against the almighty
    at the Sea of Reeds.

1: But he saved them, as he had promised,
    in order to show his great power.
    He commanded the Sea of Reeds, and it dried up,
    and he led his people across it as though on dry land.

2: He saved them from those who hated them;
    he rescued them from their enemies.
    The water drowned their enemies;
    not one of them was left.
    Then his people believed his promises,
    and sang praise to him.

1: But they quickly forgot what he had done.
    They acted without waiting for his advice.
    They were filled with desire in the desert,
    and put God to the test;
    so he gave them what they asked for,
    but sent a terrible disease among them.

2: There in the desert they were jealous of Moses,
    and of Aaron, the Lord's holy servant;
    fire came down and burned up those wicked people.

1: They made a gold calf at Horeb,
    and worshiped this image;
    they exchanged the glory of God
    for the image of an animal that eats grass.

2: They forgot the God who had saved them,
   by his mighty acts in Egypt.
   What wonderful things he did there!
   What amazing thing he did at the Sea of Reeds!

1: Then they refused the pleasant land,
   because they did not believe God's promise.
   They stayed in their tents and grumbled,
   and would not listen to the Lord.

2: They intermarried with the heathen,
   and imitated their pagan ways.
   God's people worshiped idols,
   and this caused their destruction.

1: They offered their own sons and daughters
   as sacrifices to pagan gods;
   they killed these innocent people,
   their own sons and daughters,
   as a sacrifice to the idols of Canaan;
   the land was made impure by these killings.
   They defiled themselves by their actions,
   and were unfaithful to God.

2: So the Lord was angry with his people;
   he was disgusted with them.
   He abandoned them to the power of the heathen,
   and their enemies ruled over them.
   They were oppressed by their enemies,
   and were in complete subjection to them.
   Many times the Lord rescued his people,
   but they chose to rebel against him,
   and sank deeper into sin.

1: Yet the Lord heard them when they cried out,
   and took notice of their distress.
   For their sake he remembered his covenant,
   and because of his great love he changed his mind.
   He made those who held them prisoners
   feel sorry for them.

2:   *Save us, Lord our God,*
     and bring us back

so that we may praise your holy name,
and be happy in thanking you.

L: Let us praise the Lord, the God of Israel;
   praise him now and forever!

U: *"Amen!" Praise the Lord!*

110

L: The Lord said to my lord, the king,
   "Sit here at my right side,
   until I put your enemies under your feet."

1: From Zion the Lord will extend your royal power.
   "Rule over your enemies," he says.
   The day you fight your enemies
   your people will volunteer.
   Like the dew early in the morning,
   your young men will come to you on the sacred hills.

2: The Lord made a solemn promise,
   and will not take it back;
   "You will be a priest forever,
   in the priestly order of Melchizedek."

1: The Lord is at your right side;
   he will pass judgment on the nations.

2: The king will drink from the stream by the road,
   and strengthened, he will stand victorious.

114

L: When the people of Israel left Egypt,
   when Jacob's descendants left that foreign land,
   Judah became the Lord's holy people,
   Israel became his own possession.

1: The Sea of Reeds looked and ran away,
   the Jordan River stopped flowing.
   The mountains skipped like goats,
   the hills skipped around like sheep.

2: What happened, Sea, to make you run away?
   and you, Jordan, why did you stop flowing?

Mountains, why did you skip like goats?
Hills, why did you skip around like sheep?

U: Tremble, earth, at the Lord's coming,
at the presence of the God of Jacob,
who changes rocks into pools of water,
and stone cliffs into flowing springs.

118:1

L: Give thanks to the Lord, because he is good,
and his love is eternal.

1: *Let the people of Israel say, "His love is eternal."*

2: Let the priests of God say, "His love is eternal."

U: *Let all who fear him say, "His love is eternal."*

1: In my distress I called to the Lord;
he answered me, and set me free.

2: The Lord is with me, I will not be afraid;
what can men do to me?
It is the Lord who helps me.

1: It is better to trust in the Lord
than to depend on men.
It is better to trust in the Lord
than to depend on human leaders.

2: Many enemies were around me;
but I destroyed them by the power of the Lord!
They were around me on every side;
but I destroyed them by the power of the Lord!

1: They swarmed around me like bees,
but they burned out as quickly as a brush fire;
by the power of the Lord I destroyed them!

2: *I was fiercely attacked and was being defeated,*
but the Lord helped me.
The Lord makes me powerful and strong;
he is my Savior!

L: Listen to the glad shouts of victory
in the tents of God's people;

U: *"The Lord's mighty power has done it!"*
I will not die, but I will live,
and tell what the Lord has done.

119:65

L: You have kept your promise, Lord,
and you are good to me, your servant.
Give me wisdom and knowledge,
because I trust in your commands.

1: Before you punished me I used to go wrong,
but now I obey your word.
How good you are, how kind;
teach me your commands!

2: Proud men have told lies about me,
but with all my heart I obey your rules.
These men have no understanding,
but I find pleasure in your law.

1: My punishment was good for me,
because it made me learn your commands.
The law that you give means more to me
than all the money in the world.

2: You created me, and you keep me safe;
give me understanding, so that I may learn your laws.

1: Those who fear you will be glad when they see me,
because I trust in your promise.
I know that your rules are righteous, Lord,
and that you punished me because you are faithful.

2: Let your constant love comfort me,
as you have promised me, your servant.
Have mercy on me, and I will live.

121

L: I look to the mountains; where will my help come from?

U: *My help comes from the Lord,*
who made heaven and earth.

1: May he not let me fall;
may my protector keep awake!

2: The protector of Israel does not doze or sleep!
The Lord will guard you!

1: He is by your side to protect you.
The sun will not hurt you during the day,
nor the moon during the night.

2: The Lord will protect you from all danger;
he will keep you safe.

U: *He will protect you as you come and go,*
from now on and forever.

122

L: I was glad when they said to me,
"Let us go to the Lord's house!"

1: *Now we are here,*
standing inside the gates of Jerusalem!
Jerusalem is a city restored
in beautiful order and harmony!

2: *This is where the tribes come, the tribes of Israel,*
to give thanks to the Lord, as he commanded them.
This is where the king judges his people.

1: Pray for the peace of Jerusalem!
"May those who love you prosper!
May there be peace inside your walls,
and safety in your palaces."

2: For the sake of my friends and companions,
I say to Jerusalem, "Peace be with you!"

U: *For the sake of the house of the Lord,*
our God, I pray for your prosperity.

124

L: What if the Lord had not been on our side?
Answer, Israel!

1: *"If the Lord had not been on our side,*
when our enemies attacked us,
then they would have swallowed us alive,
in their furious anger against us;

then the flood would have carried us away,
the water would have drowned us,
the raging torrent would have drowned us."

2: Let us thank the Lord,
who has not let our enemies destroy us.
We have escaped like a bird from the hunter's trap;
the trap has been broken, and we are free!

U: *Our help comes from the Lord,*
who made heaven and earth.

125

L: Those who trust in the Lord are like Mount Zion,
which can never be shaken, never be moved.

1: *As the mountains surround Jerusalem,*
so the Lord surrounds his people,
from now on and forever.

2: The wicked will not always rule
over the land of God's people;
if they did, God's people themselves might do evil.

1: *Lord, do good to those who are good,*
to those who obey your commands!

2: But punish those who follow their own wicked ways,
when you punish the evildoers!

U: *Peace be with Israel!*

127–128

L: If the Lord does not build the house,
the work of the builders is useless;

1: *if the Lord does not protect the city,*
it does no good for the sentries to stand guard.

2: It is useless to work so hard for a living,
getting up early and going to bed late,
because the Lord gives rest to those he loves.

1: Children are a gift from the Lord;
they are a real blessing.

2: Happy are those who fear the Lord,
   who live by his commands!

1: *A man who obeys the Lord will surely be blessed.*

2: May the Lord bless you from Zion!
   May you see Jerusalem prosper
   all the days of your life!

U: *Peace be with Israel!*

133

L: How wonderful it is, how pleasant,
   for God's people to live together like brothers!

1: *It is like precious olive oil running down.*

2: It is like the dew on Mount Hermon,
   falling on the hills of Zion.

U: *That is where the Lord has promised his blessing,
   life that never ends.*

136

L: Give thanks to the Lord, because he is good;

U: his love is eternal.

1: *Give thanks to the greatest of all gods;*

U: *his love is eternal.*

2: Give thanks to the mightiest of all lords;

U: his love is eternal.

1: *He alone does great miracles;*

U: *his love is eternal.*

2: By his wisdom he made the heavens;

U: his love is eternal;

1: *he built the earth on the deep waters;*

U: *his love is eternal.*

2: He made the sun and the moon;

U: his love is eternal;

1: *the sun to rule over the day;*

U: *his love is eternal;*
2: the moon and the stars to rule over the night;
U: his love is eternal.
1: *He led the people of Israel out of Egypt;*
U: *his love is eternal;*
2: with his strong hand, his powerful arm;
U: his love is eternal.
1: *He divided the Sea of Reeds;*
U: *his love is eternal;*
2: he led his people through it;
U: his love is eternal;
1: *he drowned Pharaoh and his army;*
U: *his love is eternal.*
2: He led his people in the desert;
U: his love is eternal.
1: *He killed powerful kings;*
U: *his love is eternal.*
2: He gave their land to his people;
U: his love is eternal;
1: *he gave it to Israel, his servant;*
U: *his love is eternal.*
2: He did not forget us when we were defeated;
U: his love is eternal;
1: *he freed us from our enemies;*
U: *his love is eternal.*
2: He gives food to all men and animals;
U: his love is eternal.
L: *Give thanks to the God of heaven;*
U: *his love is eternal.*

PSALMS OF
BLESSING AND SCATTERING

67:1

L: God, be merciful to us and bless us;

U: *look on us with kindness,*
that the whole world may know your will;
that all nations may know your salvation.

L: May the peoples praise you, God;

U: *may all peoples praise you!*

L: God, our God, has blessed us.

U: *God has blessed us;*
may all people everywhere honor him.

90:1

L: Lord, you have always been our home.

U: *Before the hills were created,*
e you brought the world into being,
you are eternally God, without beginning or end.

1: Fill us each morning with your constant love,
that we may sing and be glad all our life.

2: *Let us, your servants, see your mighty acts;*
let our descendants see your glorious might.

U: *Lord, our God, may your blessings be with us.*

115:15

L: May you be blessed by the Lord,
who made heaven and earth!

U: *We, the living, will give thanks to him,*
now and forever.
Praise the Lord!

121

L: I look to the mountains;
where will my help come from?

U: *My help comes from the Lord,*
who made heaven and earth.

1: May he not let me fall;
may my protector keep awake!

2: The protector of Israel does not doze or sleep!
The Lord will guard you;
he is by your side to protect you.

1: *The sun will not hurt you during the day,*
nor the moon during the night.

2: The Lord will protect you from all danger;
he will keep you safe.

U: *He will protect you as you come and go,*
from now on and forever.

125:1

L: Those who trust in the Lord are like Mount Zion,
which can never be shaken, never be moved.

U: *As the mountains surround Jerusalem,*
so the Lord surrounds his people,
from now on and forever.

L: Peace be with Israel!

128:1

L: Happy are those who fear the Lord,
who live by his commands!

U: *A man who obeys the Lord will surely be blessed.*

L: May the Lord bless you from Zion!
May you see Jerusalem prosper
all the days of your life!

U: *Peace be with Israel.*

129:8

L: "May the Lord bless you!

U: *We bless you in the name of the Lord!"*

138:1

L: I thank you, Lord, with all my heart;
I sing praise to you.

U: *You answered me when I called to you;*
with your strength you strengthened me.

L: You will do everything you have promised me;

U: *Lord, your love is constant forever.*
Complete the work that you have begun.

143:1

L: Lord, hear my prayer, listen to my plea!

U: *You are righteous and faithful, so answer me!*

L: I remember the days gone by;
I think about all that you have done,
I bring to mind all your deeds.

U: *I lift up my hands to you in prayer;*
like dry ground my soul thirsts for you.

L: I trust in you;
in the morning remind me of your constant love.

U: *My prayers go up to you;*
show me the way I should go.

L: You are my God; teach me to do your will.

U: *May your Spirit be good to me*
and guide me on a safe path.

(A. B. C) Capital letters in parentheses identify passages recommended for use in Cycles A. B. or C by the Inter-Lutheran Commission on Worship.

(a. b. c) Small letters in parentheses identify passages recommended for use in Cycles A. B. or C by the editor.

\# This symbol identifies passages recommended for use during all cycles by the Inter-Lutheran Commission on Worship.

WEEKLY CHURCH YEAR LECTIONARY

	Call to Prayer and Celebration	Praise	Call to Confession	Psalm of Confession	Assurance	Preparation for the Word	Supplication	Affirmation	Blessing and Scattering
Father									
Festival*	81	8	123:1	106:4	103:8	119:124	77	78:1	121
Fathertide 2	134	97		69:5	131	119:124	10:12	78:38	90:1
Fathertide 3	62:5	148	37:23	38:1	62:1	119:124	12	105	90:1
Reformation									
(F-4)	149:1	81	62	119:25	119:114	119:124	119:145	18:1	138:1
All Saints									
(F-5)	87:3	95:1	65:1	79:8	31:21	119:124	79	133	67:1
Fathertide 6	68:19	145:1	58:1	119:169	119:153	119:124	64	27:1	90:1
Fathertide 7	92:1	115	33:8	51:1	107:10	119:124	74	23	90:1
Thanksgiving									
(F-8)	150:1	100	50	130	65:1	119:124	54:1	20	115:15

* 8 weeks before the First Sunday in Advent.

	Call to Celebration	Praise	Call to Confession	Psalm of Confession	Assurance	Preparation for the Word	Supplication	Affirmation	Blessing and Scattering
Advent 1	122:1	3	80:1 (B)	25:1 (C)	85:1 (a, c) 91:14 (b)	119:97	73	122 (A, b) 91 (c)	143:1
2	72:18 (A) 114:7 (b) 126 (C)	145:13	4	28:1	85:1 (B) 91:14 (a, c)	119:97	72:1 (A) 85:4 (B) 6:1 (c)	106:1	129:8
3	41:10	146 (A)	7:1	130	99:8	119:97	119:81	91 (a) 122 (b, c)	90:1
4	89:1 (a, c) 145:17 (b)	24 (A, c) 89:1 (B)	14	19:12	130	119:97	80 (C)	114	121
Nativity Festival	96:7	96# 97# 98#	119:1	51:10	28:6	119:33	16	18:1	115:15
1	96:1	132 111#	15	51:10	66:16	119:33	16	125	128:1
2	66:1	147:12#	18:20	41:4	94:17	119:33	144	124	125:1
Epiphany	72:18#	67	19:7	69:5	65:1	119:33	72:1#	21:1	67:1
Baptism of Our Lord	77:1	29	2#	70	18:4	19:7	123	121	138:1
After Epiphany 2	18:31	40:1 (A) 67 (B, c)	36:1 (C)	70	18:4	19:7	141	110	67:1
3	21:13	113 (C)	80:1 (a, c) 62 (B) 1 (A, B) 119:1 (c)	40:12	28:6	19:7	119:49	27:1 (A)	67:1
4	35:9	9:1	112 (A) 119:1 (A)	19:12	55:16	19:7	71 (C)	20	67:1
5	68:32	147:1 (B)	1 (c)	38:1	31:21	19:7	85:4 (C)	125	67:1
6	84:1	119:89	41:1 (B)						
7	70:1	103:1 (A, C) 92 (b)	62 (A, c) 80:1 (b)	41:4 51:1	32 (B) 91:14	19:7 19:7	140:1 41:4 (B)	136 119:65	90:1 90:1
8	106:47	103 (a, B) 92 (c)	2 (A) 50 (B, c)	79:8	85:1	19:7	13	91	90:1
Transfiguration	68:3	99 (C)		119:124	119:114	19:7	129/130	20	90:1

WEEKLY CHURCH YEAR LECTIONARY (Cont.)

	Call to Prayer and Celebration	Praise	Call to Confession	Psalm of Confession	Assurance	Preparation for the Word	Supplication	Affirmation	Blessing and Scattering
Ash Wednesday	51:10#	84	10:1	40:12	103:8	119:137	69:1	34	143:1
Lent 1	129:1	5:1	36:1	130 (A)	103:8	119:137	6:1 (B)	91 (C)	143:1
2	116:12	115 (a, B) 42 (C)	119:17	25:1	55:16	119:137	9:13	105 (A, b) 27:1 (c)	143:1
3	40:13 (a, b) 126 (C)	137:1	94:3	38:1	131	119:137 (a, c) 19:7 (B)	142 (A) 17 (b, c)	119:65	143:1
4	34:1	43:3 (A)	27:7 (B)	119:25	32 (C)	119:137	44	27:1 (a, B) 105 (c)	143:1
5	51:10 (B)	116 (A)	52	28:1 (C)	28:6 (C)	119:137	60:1	18:1	143:1
Palm Sunday	118:19	22:22	82	119:169	31:21#	119:64	31:1#	122	138:1
Maundy Thursday	116:12#	89:1	119:114	19:12	55:16	119:64	55:12	23	67:1
Good Friday	68:19	42	49:1	79:8	103:8	119:64	22:1#	124	67:1
Festival of the Resurrection	98:1 118:19#	30 (a, b) 145:1 (c) 150 (a) 148 (B) 149 (C)	139	51:10	18:4	19:7	71	118:1#	138:1
After Easter 1	124:1	145:1 (a, b) 30 (C)	11	41:4	62:1	19:7	86	105 (A)	121
2	18:46		26	70	107:10	19:7	16 (A, c) 139 (B)	34	115:15
3	67	96	37:1	28:1	28:6	19:7	39	23#	129:8
4	66:1	33 (A) 22:22 (B) 145:1 (C)	112	51:1	66:16	19:7	56	21:1	90:1
5	96:7	66 (A) 98 (B) 67 (C)	119:33	119:124	91:14	19:7	94	127/128	125:1
(Ascension) 6	47:5#	93	27:7	40:12	130	119:41	83:1	110#	67:1

	Call to Prayer and Celebration	Praise	Call to Confession	Psalm of Confession	Assurance	Preparation for the Word	Supplication	Affirmation	Blessing and Scattering
Pentecost	68:32	104#	1	51:10	31:21	119:41	139	121	125:1
Trinity		29 (A) 149 (B) 8 (C)	75	106:4	99:8	119:41	90	27:1	121
After Pentecost	136								
2	117 (C)	81 (B)	120	19:12	31:21 (A)	119:41	31:1 (A)	27:1	125:1
3	18:1	30 (C)	50 (A) 2 (b, c)	119:124	119:14	119:64	61 (B)	91	125:1
4	100 (A)	92 (B) 107:1 (a, B) 63:1 (C)	119:161	119:169	32 (C)	119:64	59:1	118:1	125:1
5	41:10	89:1 (A) 30 (B, c)	119:9	119:25	107:10	119:64	69:1 (A)	34	125:1
6	71:22	145:13 (A)	10:1	130	18:4	119:64	16 (C)	133	125:1
7	103:19	66 (b, C)	4	28:1	28:6	119:124	143 (B)	136	128:1
8	105:1	65 (A)	7:1	25:1 (C)	55:16	119:124	85:4 (B)	119:65	128:1
9	113:1	19	15 (C)	40:12	62:1	119:124	86 (A)	23 (B)	128:1
10	118:1	138 (a, C) 145:13 (B)	11	69:5	65:1	119:124 (A)	140:1	18:1	128:1
11	121:1	104 (A)	49:1 (C)	106:4	66:16	119:137	55:1	78:1 (B)	143:1
12	34:1 (B)	33 (C)	19:7	41:4	85:1 (A)	119:137	74	78:38	143:1
13	67 (A)	34	82 (C)	51:10	94:17	119:137	88	34 (B)	143:1
14	117 (C)	138 (A)	33:8	19:12	99:8	119:137	142	91 (a, b, c) 34 (B)	143:1
15	127:1	84	26 (A) 15 (B) 112 (C)	130	32	119:97	79	106:1	138:1
16	135:1	71:1 (a, c) 146 (B) 103 (A)	119:33 (A)	119:25	103:8	119:97	10:12 (C)	21:1	138:1
17	51:10 (C)	116 (B)	37:23	51:1 (C)	107:10	119:97	119:169	105	138:1

WEEKLY CHURCH YEAR LECTIONARY (Cont.)

	Call to Prayer and Celebration	Praise	Call to Confession	Psalm of Confession	Assurance	Preparation for the Word	Supplication	Affirmation	Blessing and Scattering
After Pentecost (cont.)									
18	146:1	113 (C)	27:7 (A)	38:1	119:114	119:97	54:1 (B)	27:1 (A)	138:1
19	147:1	135 (a, B)	58:1	25:1 (A)	31:21	119:64	101/102	20	128:1
		146 (C)							
20	145:17	48 (a, b)	123:1	41:4	119:153	119:64	80 (A)	125	128:1 (B)
		95:1 (C)							
		57 (a, b)							
		111 (C)							
21	135:19	136	37:1	119:169	130	119:64	90 (B)	23 (A)	128:1
22	96:7 (A)	68:16	37:23	69:5	18:4	119:64	12	91 (B)	121 (C)
23	126 (B)	63:1 (A)	1 (A)	40:12	31:21	119:49	56	34 (C)	121
24	92:1	46 (b)	119:1 (B)	28:1	62:1	119:49	73	119:65	121
25	148:1 (C)	145:1 (C)	139	19:12	91:14	119:49	90 (A)	18:1	121
		145:13 (C)							
		107:1 (B)							
26	108:1	98 (C)	52	79:8	131 (A)	119:49	16 (B)	124	129:8
27	106:47 (a, b)	63:1 (a, c)	7:1	70	85:1	119:49	109:1	105 (A)	129:8
	68:3 (C)	111 (B)							
Christ the King (last after Pentecost)	68:3 (a, b)	95:1 (A, C)	50	40:12	28:6	119:137	10:12	21:1	67:1
	47:5 (c)	93 (B)							